The
CELEBRITY
PLAYBOOK

THE
CELEBRITY
PLAYBOOK

**The Insider's
Guide to Living
Like a Star**

Leslie Gornstein

Skyhorse Publishing

Skyhorse Publishing books may be purchased in bulk at
special discounts for sales promotion, corporate gifts,
fund-raising, or educational purposes. Special editions
can also be created to specifications. For details, contact
the Special Sales Department, Skyhorse Publishing, 307
West 36th Street, 11th Floor, New York, NY 10018 or
info@skyhorsepublishing.com.

Skyhorse® and Skyhorse Publishing® are registered
trademarks of Skyhorse Publishing, Inc.®, a Delaware
corporation.

Visit our website at www.skyhorsepublishing.com.

10 9 8 7 6 5 4 3 2 1

Library of Congress Cataloging-in-Publication Data is
available on file.

Cover design by Owen Corrigan

ISBN:978-1-62914-548-8
Ebook ISBN: 978-1-62914-901-1

Printed in China

Dedication

To JOHN, for making me better
To GLENN, for making me anything at all

CONTENTS

A Note From the Author

Everything you're about to read in this book is true.

For more than a decade, I've worked as a entertainment reporter, uncovering the strange realities of celebrity life from deep within the Hollywood hellmouth. In this book, you'll learn not what stars want you to know, but how they really live--how they stay rich, how they "raise" their kids, how they play the paparazzi game.

When I first started assembling the initial edition of this book, I figured I'd just put down all the facts and then let you read them. But then I realized that I must go further. I had an obligation to the next generation. Hollywood had been good to me, I realized. It gave me a career as a fist-shaking coal-hearted crusader of truth. And so I needed to give something back, not only to my readers, but to the celebrity community that spawned me.

So I packaged my arcane knowledge not in expose form, but rather in a handy handbook format. And just in time for the next generation of would-be megastars. Now they, too, can study the black art of A-listery. And, by reading this book, so can you. Ever dream of hanging out with Taylor Swift at her home in Rhode Island, cackling wildly from her window as her security people harass the beachgoers again? You'll need all the coaching you can get.

You're welcome.

Are you ^

~~Is This Book~~

Right For ~~You?~~

^*this book?*

Sorry, *The Celebrity Playbook* is RESERVED. True film stars only past this point.

If you are not a A-list celebrity—or, at the very least, a Miley Cyrus type who is expected to leer and strip her way to that peak status any second now—you should close this book immediately.[1] Otherwise the very facts within may cause your second-rate day-player eyeballs to melt, just like that grinning Nazi in *Raiders of the Lost Ark.* In fact, feel free to consider this book the Ark of the Covenant of celebritydom, minus the winged cherubim and the flesh-eating light of Yahweh. If it finds you unworthy, I cannot guarantee the safety of your face.

If you are an actual major movie star, this book is your new best friend. It contains dozens of simple, comprehensive action plans that will carry you through any crisis you might encounter as a member of the Hollywood elite. Velvet-rope ambushes, paparazzi ground assaults, a sudden two-pound weight-gain—with this book in your fiercely manicured hands, nothing can scare you anymore.

---

[1] **Confidential to Ms. Theron:** I have no idea whether you're still on the A-list or not. Stop calling me.

> **First,** a simple test, kind of like your first screen test, way back when you were just a starry-eyed porker in a pair of size-four Gap jeans.[2] If you pass, you may proceed to the next chapter. Ms. Witherspoon, if you happen to be reading this, we do not presume to judge you, the bona fide A-lister. Rather, consider this a barrier against impostors—Kardashians, cat memes, Instagram stars.

Don't worry about actually putting little checks in these checkboxes; it isn't your job to carry "stencicles" or whatever those plastic writing instruments are called. That's for your assistant to wrangle with.

☐ **1** You command, or have commanded at one point in your career, at least $15 million per film. Or, OK, $10 million, as long as you also once demanded a percentage of gross ticket receipts. Nobody routinely scores that kind of quid these days, but if your agent is still dreaming of a return to those heady times, you're probably famous enough.

☐ **2** You have graced the Vanity Fair Hollywood issue at least once, most likely in some iconic Annie Leibovitz portrait where you either stand, triumphant, on a beach, or pal around, triumphant, next to Judd Apatow or J.J. Abrams, or soak, triumphant, in an antique bathtub.

☐ **3** You can, in the words of Hollywood's more delightfully decrepit citizens, open a picture. In other words, people come to movies to see you—not the character you're playing, such as Superman, or the concept, such as "Oh My God, There Are Vampires In Alaska."

☐ **4** You have the power to "green-light" any project. If you even hint at *maybe* wanting to make a movie, a giant pile of money instantly materializes outside your production office. Film financiers live to execute your every whim, no matter how silly. Just ask your co-producer on *Planetoid!: The Musical.*

☐ **5** You have a standing invitation to Clooney's villa on Lake Como. You would come and stay, except that you have your own pied-à-terre just outside Florence.

☐ **6** You have at least two personal assistants, one who stands at your left hand, and another who stays at

[2] **You've burned** those by now, right? If not, have one of the nannies cut them up and make a tent for your children.

home and keeps your A-list children amused with organically grown spirulina smoothies and trips to the chiropractor. This second assistant is not to be confused with your personal chef, who is not to be confused with your nutritionist.

☐ **7** You may or may not own your own private plane; your publicist will neither confirm nor deny. Your publicist is also your BFF (forever and ever). That statement? Just now? Where she would neither confirm nor deny? She did that for free, just because you called her your best friend in your Oscar speech, and also because she was a bridesmaid in your second wedding.

☐ **8** You are often mistaken for a large Little League player when disguised in a baseball cap. That's because you and the large Little Leaguer

both weigh about the same: 109 pounds or thereabouts. Those aren't Adderalls in your handbag. They're *vitamins.*

☐ **9** Your asking price for endorsement deals is in the millions—similar to your per-film fee. You can model for a couture house, or you can star in a crappy blockbuster about flame-headed aliens who live in the sun and attack Earth. Being an A-lister, the choice is always yours.

☐ **10** You are invited to the Oscars every year, even when you aren't nominated. Afterward you attend supersecret post-Oscar parties so super and secret that no press is invited. Not even *Vogue*'s André Leon Talley, who is just so fabulous.

☐ **11** You aren't really reading this. Your assistant or other assistant is reading it aloud to you.

☐ **12** Your agent got you a galley of this book four months before it was published. That way you could snap up the movie rights before Shia LaBeouf could, that punk. And by the way, thanks so much for the generous offer, but I've already optioned the script to Sam Raimi.

George Clooney. His villa es su villa.

---

[3] **Kidding!** The option is still for sale, Mr. LaBeouf. I won't even ask for final creative approval. And, by the way, you may have noticed that I am now addressing you despite my previous ban on B-listers. That's because I am confident that your participation in *The A-List Playbook: The Motion Picture* will rocket you to the very top of the A-List!

The
CELEBRITY
PLAYBOOK

Why You Had to Pay For This Book

For you, the A-lister, this is not just a book. It is a career-saving necessity. It just might be the only document standing between you and *Dancing With the Stars*.

If you had to pay for this book, either full price or even with a celebrity discount, I apologize on behalf of the mouth breathers at my publishing house. If it helps at all, they're not from Los Angeles. They don't know that you, as an A-lister, rarely have to pay for such incidentals as books.

Still, I can guarantee that this book is worth every penny your assistant had to pay on your behalf. The techniques you are about to read have all been tested by real stars, just like you. I have spent years gathering these tools as a celebrity journalist, documenting every detail of the A-list lifestyle in magazines, newspapers, and online outlets. I have gathered inside strategies for planning million-dollar weddings—and intimate, $500,000 second weddings—as well as celebrity baby showers, vacations, swag suite expeditions, movie press junkets, and red-carpet forays. As the resident question-and-answer columnist for *Yahoo!*, I have tapped into the inner workings of your everyday life:

My brain holds the keys to your survival.

And it's worth exactly the PRICE OF THIS BOOK.

CHAPTER ONE

Your People

Person husbandry—maintaining your brood of agents, stylists, bodyguards, and the like—is not a learned skill, but rather a body of knowledge. It takes years of patient observation, stern discipline, and, of course, a happy willingness to sue the disobedient. Luckily for you, your shambling elders in the acting community have spent decades and decades in this business, perfecting, in the process, much of the art of handling Hollywood minions. Thanks to their dedication, as well as this fearless guide, you, too, can recruit only the most sycophantic stylists while simultaneously keeping your agents suitably twitchy and paranoid. That's what this chapter is all about, plus so much more.

Assistants:
The Best Friends You'll Ever Pay

A-list stardom requires at least one assistant; many of your A-list peers have boasted three or even more. Aside from the obvious benefits they bring to the festival of you, assistants also make adequate best friends in a pinch. However, never doubt that your assistant has private ambitions—dreams that do not include sating your 2 AM cravings for lobster thermidor or cleaning the placenta out of your bathtub after your at-home water delivery. (Yep, assistants have been asked to do that.) Some assistants may instead have their eyes on acting or singing or seducing your secretly gay spouse or some other fanciful lost cause.

Still others wish to become producers. In that case, you have little to fear. Drew Barrymore's producing partner is a former musician's assistant. And Virginia Madsen allowed her assistant to matriculate to partner in her production company, and nothing much, bad or good, has happened to her since.

No matter what your assistant's personality—whether it be simpering or fawning—some elements of care, feeding, and sleep deprivation remain mandatory. Here's what you need to know.

Bestowing the Blessing: Hiring a New Assistant

Your fellow A-listers often face a significant challenge in seeking new personal assistants. The assistants must possess crack communication and bullying skills; a sunny attitude with a healthy dose of self-hatred; and a never-ending fascination with re-gifted lip-glosses and clothing. Some stars approach staffing agencies, such as The Help Co., which interview and screen candidates on the client's behalf. Others use semisecret headhunters so elite they require a referral before you can even approach them. Much of the time, word of mouth will dictate your next hire.

If all of your friends have already left for the Montreal Film Festival, and you have no one to give you any personal recommendations, no worries. Many stars, such as Beyoncé have plucked assistants from their own family tree; cousins and siblings carry the added benefit of family obligation, so go ahead and cut their salaries by 10 percent. (You won't have been the first celebrity to do this. You won't be the last.) Or you might try dipping into the pool of gofers who dash around every movie set. Other celebrities simply poach their assistants from their agents' offices. If one of the wispy worker bees there does an excellent job of fetching you air lattes whenever you visit the giant white marble ice floe known as CAA, then go ahead and offer that child a job.

Or try the concierge desk at The Four Seasons. Don't ask them to find you an assistant. Just hire the guy behind the desk. Concierges from that A-lister mecca say it's not uncommon for them to field job offers from celebrities right there, especially when the concierges are trapped behind their little plinths and have almost no means of escape.

Whatever route you choose, avoid growing overly attached to your new helpmate. The average employment span for a Hollywood assistant seems to be two years or less. According to surveys, plenty of former assistants often complain that they were worked too hard, were underpaid or verbally abused, or were asked to commit unspecified illegal acts on behalf of their employers. But let's be honest: the real reason for these brief tenures probably has less to do with self-serving claims of indentured servitude and more to do with the laws of physics: tiny satellites locked in tight orbits around a brilliant star are bound to get a little singed.

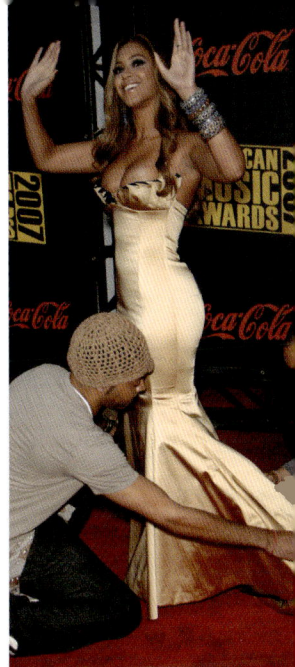

Queen Bey with her loving minions.

★★★★A-List Tip

What Not to Pay Your Assistant

According to the latest available numbers, the salary for a Hollywood personal assistant averages around $61,000 annually. (By contrast, the median salary of a mine foreman in the United States is between $66,000 and $67,000.) However, salaries range from a high of $105,000 to a low of $30,000. If you fear you are overpaying your assistant, simply reduce her salary. Keep reducing it until it hits $30,000. You may never reach that point, however; if she begins starving herself in an effort to save on food costs, she may eventually faint one too many times, failing to get up even when you order her to do so. Theoretically, you may then fire her for insubordination.

Emergency Scenario:

When the Assistant Starts Thinking

Congratulations on the baiting and capture of your new personal assistant. Now all you have to do is keep her obedient. It may not be easy. Too much lenience can create an uppity and willful helot. One day you're handing your assistant unwanted freebies from your Grammy Awards gift basket, and the next, she's sputtering crazy talk about health benefits and your husband's so-called "sexual harassment."

There's good news. Your forebears in the Legend Community have spent decades perfecting techniques for keeping assistants pliant and efficient. Below please find a list of sample assistant-related crises commonly encountered by A-list celebrities, followed by real-life solutions.

Crisis ONE

Your assistant wants to go home and rest after only eleven hours of work.

Solution: Assure her that you know her pain—you yourself often have to report for hair and makeup at an ungodly 6 AM—but together, there's nothing the two of you can't accomplish! Then instruct her to pick up those new Dior sandals for you over at that place you like.

ABSOLUTELY REAL HOLLYWOOD FACT: More than half of celebrity assistants have said they are on call twenty-four hours a day.

Crisis TWO

Your assistant has he beady eyes on that free cel phone you just scored from an awards-show gift bag You prefer your free, Swarovsk crystal-studded BlackBerry and were planning to regift the phone to your assistant. But ther she started actually asking for it. Not cool.

Solution: Think about something else.

ABSOLUTELY REAL HOLLYWOOD FACT: These days, most stars supply a computer and a cell phone to their personal assistants, along with a company credit card they can use to buy stuff on your behalf Also, at least 80 percent of personal assistants regularly get hand-me-downs from their bosses' gift bags. May as well give your assistant the phone. Just make sure to warn her not to ask for anything else After all, there are people starving in .. somewhere.

---

[4] **This is strictly** a theoretical example. Please insert your own pet cause above.

Your assistant keeps whining something about the rust holes on her car and how she can't afford to fix them, something about having to buy her own food.

Crisis THREE

Solution: A-listers have been known to gift their assistants with a vacation or new car or some other sop when the little helpers start to wilt. So maybe you pay for her car repairs and then have your publicist leak the humanity-affirming story to a magazine or blog. **ABSOLUTELY REAL HOLLYWOOD FACT:** Most stars such as yourself provide their assistants with health insurance, an annual bonus, and about two weeks' vacation. It's also expected that you pay; average annual pay is about is about $60,000. But Then again, almost half of all Hollywood assistants who want a pay raise must first ask for one. Because your assistant never whined about anything specific like "weekly salary" or "raises," the car-repair money should be considered more than enough.

Your assistant would like to fly first-class.

Crisis FOUR

Solution: That's cute. It thinks it's people. You may be kind of screwed here, as most assistants and their employers see first-class flunky travel as a long-established norm. Go ahead and put up your assistant in style, and leak the sensational details to a friendly media scribe. Make it absolutely clear to your assistant that speaking to the press is your publicist's job, not your assistant's, because …

ABSOLUTELY REAL HOLLYWOOD FACT: …Nearly all celebrity personal assistants must sign sweeping nondisclosure agreements before reporting for their first day of work.

Your assistant has balked at your request that she please take this stool sample to your doctor, and that while she's at it, pick up some porn on the way home.

Crisis FIVE

Solution: Yeesh, what is her problem? Both of those requests—transporting the stool sample and transporting porn—are not new. In fact both have been mentioned as very real experiences in a survey[2] conducted by the Association of Celebrity Personal Assistants. So were picking the client's dog's nose, filming the birth of a client's first child, purchasing illegal drugs, and attending traffic school while posing as the boss. **ABSOLUTELY REAL HOLLYWOOD FACT:** All of those things above are facts.

---

[5] **No celebrity names** were disclosed in the survey. But if you see yourself in any of these anecdotes, wave at yourself!

Emergency Scenario:

You Have No Idea How to Fill a Prescription.

Breathe in. Breathe out. You are not alone. Celebrities suffer these kinds of very real crises all the time. Maybe you, say, just fired your assistant, and now you have no idea how to get your Klonopin, I mean, vitamins. Hopefully you have some vitamins in your system when you first realized your error. If not, bum a vitamin off of your trainer and take a few minutes for it to kick in.

Now you can think.

The question remains: How can you, a public figure, get your prescriptions filled without the contents of your medicine cabinet being leaked to the press? Here's how it's done.

In most cases, stars find doctors willing to write them prescriptions under a pseudonym. (Not a pseudonym for the doctor, a pseudonym for you. *Don't be alarmed: fuzzy thinking is a known side effect of vitamins.*) The late Anna Nicole Smith reportedly sought her prescriptions under the guise of one "Michelle Chase," while Michael Jackson preferred Omar Arnold, Joseph Scruz and Bill Bray. But as a member of the Hollywood creative community, really, you can do better than that.

The California Health and Safety Code dictates that no one who prescribes or dispenses a controlled substance can put a phony name or address on the prescription. In fact, the California Health and Safety Code states that the prescriber can't enhance the prescription form with any creative embel-

lishment whatsoever. Then again, as celebrity defense attorneys have claimed, the onus of those laws falls squarely on your doctor. And because his practice is *clearly* enhanced by your patronage, he should be more than eager to take the fall for you. So, back to your new pseudonym!

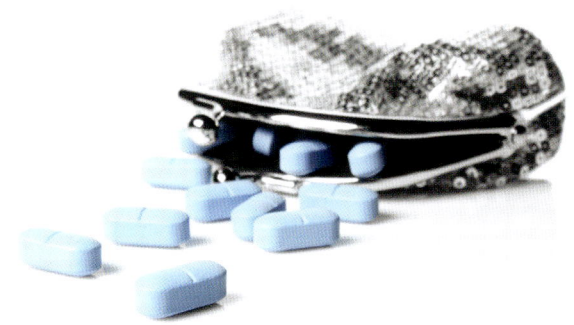

Avoid the temptation to express yourself too much in this otherwise fairly creative exercise. A name that reflects a part of who you are (e.g., Martinique de la Tragically Misunderstood) may offer inner satisfaction on a small level, but arousing the suspicion of the drones at Walgreens really isn't worth it.

Instead, consider a name that will not elicit suspicion. Maybe you go with a name that evokes a living legend—someone at least eighty years old who is used to a certain level of luxury and isn't keen on being questioned. (For starters: The Baroness Elsa Von Vaderheim.) Stretch your creative skills and imagine someone who is the total opposite of you—although within the same gender, just in case a tetchy pharmacist starts asking too many questions—and name that imaginary person. Then no one will figure you out. Say your exact opposite is a poor, lunk-headed gas station attendant who enjoyed his prime in 1950s Milwaukee. In that case, you might go for a Francis "Happy" McGee or a Buzz Del Vecchio. Whatever you choose, have several workable backups ready. Because... editor: set as "ABSOLUTELY REAL HOLLYWOOD FACT".

Creating a Stage Name for
Prescription Purposes

Never underestimate the power of a good fake name. A nondescript nom de prescription can take you a long way in arranging your illicit romantic rendezvous with Monsieur Vicodin and his suave wingman, Señor Xanax, but the alias is useless if it arouses suspicion from law enforcement or a pharmacist. Take care with your fake prescription name. Create a whole character for it if it helps. Here are a few suggested names to get you started. As of press time, none were taken.

The Rev. Elias Krowther—a man of God whose name evokes a more innocent era, back when battles had names and everybody trusted everybody. Definitely a winner.

Dahlia Cortez—exudes old Hollywood glamour, yet ethnically indistinct. Could be an ancient silent movie star. Could be a clerk at Rite Aid.

Xavier Laderoot—a common name among the French Canadian population; excellent alias if you are shooting on location in Quebec or if you are visiting your good friend Brad Pitt in New Orleans.

Chris Brown—No one has gotten into an argument with anyone bearing that name since 2009.

John Christopher Depp II—*Could that be . . . no way. Johnny Depp? That's his real name, so . . . OMG Dahlia, quit filling that bullshit Valtrex prescription and look at this.* While the pharmacists are busy debating over whether to call Page Six about Captain Jack's possible Oxycontin hang-up, you may run off, cackling, with your floaty tabs.

Your Entourage & You:
What You Need to Know About Your Human Barricade

psychic

security

attorney

You

assistant

publicist

dancer

girlfriends

Your circle of
(paid) friends.

A proper entourage is critical to maintaining one's allure as a star. However, entourages also have many practical purposes not directly associated with your self-luminescence. Mark Wahlberg managed to parlay his entourage into a hit TV show, and the Kardashians are wizards at using their slightly-fatter hangers-on to make themselves look intelligent and beautiful. But the options for exploiting your people absolutely do not end there. For example, entourages also make excellent human shields. It's much easier to separate oneself from the unfortunates in the general population when one is surrounded by trustworthy people of an appropriate jeans size. Even a size-zero wardrobe stylist can make a fine human buffer when girded by several more of her kind. Do not be afraid to put your stylist on the front lines; she would easily take a bullet for you, even if she hasn't said so.

At first, you may think you need an entourage that matches your pay grade — say, 20. After all, this was the size of the entourage described by SNL actor Bill Hader, after he survived an SNL episode with egg-throwing man child Justin Bieber. [subscript]6

Or maybe you only want go semi-diva. That's cool. If Jennifer Lopez can do a photo shoot with only, say, five people around—and she has—you can too.

But if you dream of living like a real A-lister these days, think smaller. Per Hader, Justin Timberlake, who is definitely several rungs above Bieber, tends to show up to his SNL gigs with maybe one other flunky at the most.

But if you still think you need an entourage, no worries. It is easy and even fun to muster a Maginot line of sycophants if you approach the task with the proper spirit.

Your recruitment pool is larger than you think. According to the world's most experienced bouncers, typical draftees include:

Adrian Grenier: Looking lost (and significantly less handsome) without his homely band of bros standing behind him. Bet he's missing the good old days.

Justin Bieber, all grown up and ready to be tried as an adult.

---

[6] **Hader** Hader once told Howard Stern: "Justin Bieber showed up with like 20 guys. And every time, backstage is a very small constructed place, he had a guy holding a slice of pizza, a guy holding a Diet Coke. You were trying to fight around all these people to get dressed."

- Agents
- Attorneys[7]
- Makeup artists
- Security personnel[8]
- Your personal financial advisor
- Fellow band or cast members
- Protégé MCs[9]
- Producers

- People from 'round the way or back in the day (but never both)
- Backup dancers
- Publicists[10]
- Assistant publicists
- Kristen Stewart. She once hung out in Katy Perry's entourage, so.
- Girlfriends

- Girlfriends of the girlfriends, who may, if you are a straight man and very lucky, be sleeping with the previously mentioned girlfriends—but, either way, will soon be sleeping with you, if they wish to remain in your posse.

Recruiting Hair and Wardrobe Stylists

You may have noticed that the recruitment list above does not include hair gurus or wardrobe stylists. Both species can make excellent entourage members. Even though they are technically on the clock while having that cup of coffee with you, if you're promoting a movie or other project, your movie studio or record label will usually pick up the tab. And here's a

bonus: Stylists are excellent at walking just slightly ahead of you when entering a room, making you look precisely as important as you actually are.

However, proceed with caution. Recently, hair and wardrobe stylists have begun to get as much ink as their clients. Case in point: hairstylist Ken Paves and his client Jessica Simpson. This may work for middling stars like Simpson, who falls somewhere between C-lister and Miss Clearfield County. Also,

[7] **Suge Knight** has been spotted out and about with his attorneys. Suge isn't an A-lister, of course. Unless he's reading this right now, in which case, Mr. Knight, you are the most legendary human being to join the entertainment community since Sinatra!

[8] But not just any security personnel. For more on recruiting a bodyguard, see page 34.

[9] This possibility refers to rappers only. A thespian should never have protégé MCs, even if the actor spits fine game.

[10] Publicists are among the finest recruits for entourages because they often mistake themselves for your friends and therefore will accompany you almost anywhere with little to no advance notice. For more on publicists, see page 58.

before Kim Kardashian shot the sex tape that would launch an empire, she had a gig as a personal stylist to folk like Brandy.

That's fine for some. But nobody steps on an A-lister's glitter. Keep your posse in check; never allow them to appear on a red carpet with you. This leniency usually leads to a reality show for the stylist, and having a reality TV star in your entourage automatically dims your star power by a 10 to 15 order of magnitude. Those numbers are an estimate. The threat to your stardom is not.

Lady Gaga knows that in order to stand out on the red carpet you have to ditch your entourage, and sometimes the only way to do that is to threaten them with a sharp and inexplicable accessory.

Emergency Scenario:
Your Posse Is Still Too Small

Suppose your entourage is still wallowing in the five-to-six-person range, and you're craving a more Bieber-esque number. In those cases, it is acceptable to recruit a hungry young climber of no particular pedigree.[11] However, one must take extra care during the early phases of introduction and indoctrination. The best way to train your youngling is to make him watch your car while *you up in the club*.

According to bouncers, A-list celebrities routinely shun valet parking, choosing instead to have their car idling nearby. (A-listers do not wait for valets, and most, being big on control, do not employ drivers and prefer to motor about themselves.) As such, a trustworthy and alert person must watch the car to ensure it does not get towed. Bouncers say this is typically the job of the new posse recruit. Should the young hopper succeed in watching the car while *you up in the club*, and do it several times without complaint or flaw, you may promote the scrub into the main body of the entourage at your own discretion.

[11] This act, while selfless, does not count as charity work for tax purposes. Budget accordingly.

Police Officers as Entourage: Twisting the Long Arm of the Law

With just a little extra effort, you can trick police officers into joining your entourage. For obvious reasons, peace officers make excellent last-minute, temporary posse members. They provide added safety and an air of authority that can strike fear into smaller or more highly strung members of the press.

Of course, most cops, even the not-fat ones, would normally make for reluctant fawning hangers-on. Here's where the aforementioned "trick" comes into play. With just a little bit of celebrity feng shui, you can attract cops to your side without so much as shots being fired. The most effective means of inviting a police entourage to join your crew requires a storefront business located in a celebrity-friendly area (West Hollywood works). Small restaurants and boutiques rank among the best staging areas. In any event, the business must have a sidewalk front entrance and large picture windows.

Arrive at the business and settle yourself in for a small "lunch," ensuring that you are radiating your positive celebrity "chi" near one of the large sidewalk-facing windows. While you enjoy your hot mug of organic air with a side of lemon water, watch the front windows. Paparazzi will eventually converge, not unlike algae gunk on a fish tank (especially if your publicist has done her job and tipped them off).

Once the sidewalk clogs with perhaps twenty paparazzi, the business owner or restaurant manager will likely call the authorities, citing a public safety disaster and requesting help in dispersing the hazardous lens vermin. Local safety ordinances require that sidewalks remain clear and unobstructed. According to law enforcement experts, a typical deployment in this case calls for a single police vehicle containing *two* officers. However, in your case, A-Lister, expect at least triple that, along with any or all of the following: a police helicopter, a motorcycle unit, a K9 squad, and (if you are Britney Spears) a special police mental health unit.

Reporters or crybaby watchdog groups may later blast the police response as overkill, a disgusting example of celebrity favoritism, and an unconscionable taxpayer expense. You *alone* will know the truth: Fame is the deadliest disease of all, worse than rickets, scarlet fever, and that thing that makes your nose fall off, *combined*. You are sick and you need your medicine—in this case, a delightfully pugnacious battery of uniformed cops to conspicuously shove the brazen paps into the gutter, where they *belong* (until the next time you need them).

A public lunch outing by middling star Nicole Richie once attracted a clutch of fewer than two dozen paparazzi in West Hollywood. According to an eyewitness, the sheriff's office responded with five law enforcement officers in three cars.

During Britney's second transport to a hospital for mental health issues, police deployed at least a dozen LAPD motorcycles and squad cars, one helicopter, a special mental heath unit, and an ambulance.[12] Cost estimates for the operation ranged from $10,000 to $25,000. In planning the convoy, police cited the more than one hundred trailing paparazzi as a potential danger.[13]

Since then, a horde of other stars, many suitable to be seen with you, have sung the praises of police escorts. In Washington D.C. alone, roughly 17 celebs have enjoyed police escorts, including Justin Timberlake, Taylor Swift, Jay-Z and Christina Aguilera. Also on that list: Charlie Sheen, who once Tweeted, "[In] car with Police escort in front and rear! [D]riving like someone's about to deliver a baby! Cop car lights #Spinning!"

Yes, technically, police escorts in D.C. are supposed to be reserved for presidents and such, and your promoter may have to reimburse the police department for the expense, but it's worth it.

Once your police entourage has assembled, be sure to treat them with extra deference. A kind word can come back to you threefold next time you face a DUI arrest and mutter something unfortunate about Jews. Leaks notwithstanding, no one will work harder to suppress inconvenient information with more gusto than your friends in the police force.

Taylor Swift works her magic.

[12] **Typical police** escorts call for one cop car per ten civilian vehicles.

[13] **Paparazzi** camera straps, when rubbed too quickly on your delicate skin, can cause painful "Indian burn."

Emergency Scenario:

Your Posse Is Too Large

Take a deep breath and tell yourself: *This always happens to people who carry such a bright inner light*. Without you, your poor entourage would probably be lost, living off Jim Beam fumes and whatever cash they could scrounge from a life of smash-and-grab crime. They crave your constant inspiration; be gentle with them. Take another deep breath and remind yourself that Beyoncé reportedly has traveled with an entourage of eighty. Will Smith, for his part, has traveled with so many escorts that four cars were required for transport. While visiting Israel to give a concert, Paul McCartney was said to have brought no fewer than 100 hangers-on with him, taking up 21 hotel suites in the process. And according to a report in the *Guardian*, a London paper, the production team required to handle a 2006 photo shoot with Victoria Beckham and Katie Holmes numbered about 300. Learn from less recognizable people. If Jay-Z—who may be a very snappy rapper but never earned $20 million for an acting gig in his life—can face

this kind of crisis, so can you. And he has.

Jay-Z once found himself standing outside a London club surrounded by an entourage of fifteen. The club denied him entry, citing his impressive but nonetheless way-too-large retinue.

Jay-Z simply smiled, said he understood, and promised to return someday. This was a masterstroke. In subsequent press, Jay-Z (a) managed to look like a nice young man who nonetheless (b) boasts an eighty-three-foot-long posse. And thus the circle was squared. Well-played, Jay-Z.

Jay-Z. And Hove looked upon his 30-mile-long entourage, and saw that it was ballin'.

You and Your
Massive Shadow:
All About Bodyguards

Most megastars have traveled with bodyguards at some point or another. You should have at least one on call in every major city, in case a native decides to test the tabloid theory that you are "just like us" and attempt to approach you.

Always tell your assistant to tell your manager to tell your staffing agency to select a bodyguard with care. A lumbering, easily disgruntled bodyguard may end up selling your most private details, such as your favorite Starbucks frappuccino flavor or your favorite gay swinging partner, to a tabloid.

Conversely, a small, subtle bodyguard may come with impressive referrals from your dear friend Gloria Estefan but be so tiny that he can bring no prestige to your entourage. There's no point in having people if other people don't know you have people.

Bodyguards generally fall under two categories, one clearly more desirable than the other. Make sure you are well familiar with the distinction before signing off on a hire.

Type I: The Club Cube

Your younger, tipsier colleagues in the Hollywood pantheon—and musicians—tend to recruit their bodyguards from the bouncer corps at elite nightclubs, or through friends of friends. These guards usually resemble large cubes of beef or pork and go by a nickname with the word Big in front of it, such as Big Rob, Big Mo, Big Shorty, or Big E,

who once bodyguarded for Celine Dion. Club Cubes usually boast little to no formal training—unless you count expelling drunks in Samoan bars as training[12]—but they do boast the occasional defensive driving course or criminology degree. You can spot a Club Cube from his telltale football-player build, insulated inside a comforting cocoon of endomorphic blubber. What's really important are the aesthetics—that the fat and muscle come together to form a large and well-defined square.

Choose a bodyguard with care. Big hefty ones can be fun, but they don't carry the prestige of a former Secret Service goon.

Advantages: Club Cubes cost nearly nothing, grinning and clapping their meaty hands at the notion of earning a few hundred bucks per day. They are usually content to live in the pool house or over the garage, and consider themselves on call, ready to pull themselves up on their mastodon-like legs the second you need to get wasted over at Justin Bieber's place. Great lovers of T-shirts, Club Cubes will not demand extra petty cash for fancy suits or shoes. Their well-fed presence radiates "back off" without a word. Their stored fat can provide bursts of energy when a paparazzo arrives and you need a menacing figure to leap into the photos, glaring and groping at the lens with a bearlike protectiveness usually reserved for autocratic statesmen at G8 summits.

Disadvantages: Club Cubes often forget that they work for you and may start describing themselves as your "friend." (Where Club Cubes pick up such notions is a mystery; you yourself only called Big Tommy your friend once, when he had to run down to your stylist's place at 3 AM to pick up your "vitamins.") Club Cubes also have little to no formal security training and may be

---

[14] **Wilmer Valderrama** has worked with a Club Cube known only as Tadao, who "cut his teeth bouncing drunks from Samoan bars in Carson, Calif.," per *Entertainment Weekly*.

Kimye knows that the constant presence of a protective hulking manbeast is where the party's at.

too slow to waddle in front of an incoming autograph seeker. Club Cubes love to threaten the press. They also love to call the press later and apologize and ask how much money they can get for the occasional scoop.

Most importantly, Club Cubes evoke a distinct whiff of B-listery. Because they are popular with younger, less discriminating stars, they carry the risk of blemishing your image just by standing there. Bottom line: Avoid Club Cubes unless absolutely necessary.

Type II: (Former) Secret Agent Men

Secret Agent Man comes via an elite security agency, one that employs only former British Secret Service types, Israeli commandos, or other feverishly trained defenders of freedom. Secret Agent Man has a small, compact build, moves in quick, sharp bursts, and may, in his nondescript gray suit, actually be part squirrel. You've always wanted to ask him, but you can't see him. He can scan a rooftop and all points of entry or exit in four seconds or less—even in Armani sunglasses, which can be way, way dark. Secret Agent Man also has an impressive collection of sunglasses, though, of course, unlike you, he had to pay for his.

Secret Agent Man does not disclose his clients. However, Secret Agent Man is no match for Jaded Investigative Gossip Author, who can confirm that David and Victoria Beckham, Gwyneth Paltrow, and Ben Affleck all have hired this type of security man in moments of fear.

Advantages: Secret Agent Man has no use for categories like "advantages" and "disadvantages." You can save that talk for your flabby civilian friends.

Disadvantages: *What part of "has no use for categories" don't you understand?*
Unlike a Club Cube, who thinks he's flossing high at two bills a day, Secret Agent Man starts at $200 *an hour*. Secret Agent Man will not let you drive your own car,[15] allow you to deviate from pre-approved routes, or speak to anyone who has not submitted to a background check. Secret Agent Man loathes Big Tommy. And Secret Agent Man won't party. But then again, only Type II can spot a sniper through one-way glass in complete darkness.

---

[15] **See more** about car travel on page 104.

CHAPTER TWO

Your Looks
Fashion, Beauty, and Other Absolute Essentials

Before every major awards show, emissaries from luxury companies gather in hotel suites and high-end salons, lovingly lay out their wares, and tremble with the hope that they might have the honor of treating you to a free beauty service. Nothing makes these humble craftsmen happier than seeing your already-flawless skin stabbed into a plump stupor by a free Botox treatment, your buttery locks gleaming from a free blowout by Frederic Fekkai or Patrick Melville, your assistant laden with thousands of dollars' worth of lotions and makeup that the companies have picked out just for legends like you. It is their way of saying "thank you" for elevating the state of The Arts. And also for elevating the state of their brands, which now bask in the reflected glow of your newly glass-smooth, wholly immobile forehead.

But sometimes you must take personal responsibility for your looks and fashion choices. A few of the most crucial examples are listed below.

Your Handbag:

A Patent Leather Blockade Between You and the Forces of Chaos

An A-list status does require an A-list handbag. And that means a big handbag.

Behind your back, random people may snicker at the cavernous proportions of your big, beautiful Birkin. Never mind them. There are people who have to pay for their own Birkins. They don't get their accessories as gifts from big studios and producers and publicists and agents the way you routinely do.

So: Why do you need such a massive bag? Let's start with your merciless work hours. Your schedule leaves you no choice but to throw more emergency supplies in a handbag.

Worried about the camera adding 10 pounds? A huge-ass bag will make you look tiny by comparison.

The hardy, squat folk who pay full price to see your films at the Googleplex tend to work only eight to twelve hours per day. But as a member of the Hollywood A-list, you often must soldier through fourteen-to-eighteen-hour days, roughing it on the set with nothing but a personal chef, a catering service, and

Also: Pashmina shawls simply don't fit in a Judith Leiber evening clutch.

two assistants to keep you upright. Sudden attacks of lip dryness and loneliness can emerge at any time.[16] Those attacks call for lip balm, lip gloss, lip conditioner, and at least three communication devices on your person at all times. Your lifestyle also leaves you vulnerable to sudden drafts, particularly when no one on the private jet can figure out the thermostat on trans-Atlantic flights.

That's where your leviathan-sized handbag comes into play. It can carry everything you need and then some. On the following pages, I provide a simple list of what a typical A-lister like you tends to have in her purse:

---

[16] **Not to be confused** with dehydration or exhaustion. See glossary entry on page 165.

 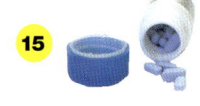

A-Lister's Survival Kit:

Everything you need to have a well-stocked handbag...for all of those "emergency" situations

1. Your cell phone. 2. Your other cell phone. Celebrity insiders say stars routinely carry two to three cell phones. Because you just need them, that's why. And also because you like to separate business contacts from personal contacts from super, super personal contacts. **3. Your** OTHER other cell phone. Ideal for making last-minute leaks about rivals—or yourself—to *Star* magazine. Also fine for taking the occasional selfie or two, but keep those to a minimum. The last thing you need is to be mistaken for Rihanna. **4. Admiral Beezus Kirby McCheekyPuffs.** Who's a good boy? Admiral Beezus Kirby McCheekyPuffs, that's who! Yes! Yes you are! **5. That Adderall that you don't have a prescription for.** It's not *your* Adderall, of course. As you're willing to tell any officer who stops you and asks, you're simply holding on to it for your manager. There is no need to inform your manager about this ahead of time. He only has one strike right now anyway. **6. The Chanel sunglasses. 7. The vintage 1973 Chanel sunglasses. 8. The vintage 1982 Chanel sunglasses.** As a practitioner of the creative arts, you never know when you might need to make a sudden change. Your life coach told you that. Or maybe it was your good friend Johnny Depp. His sunglasses are always so inspiring. **9. Lip gloss. 10. Lip tint. 11. Lip conditioner. 12. Lip balm. 13. A small, digital video camera** for documenting cases of paparazzi and stalker harassment. Just in case your cell phone camera is already filled with photos from Stella McCartney's green-themed housewarming. **14. Your "vitamins,"** which only *look* like Adderall. **15. A small shiv.** Eva Mendes reportedly used to pack a knife, after she made her first big-budget actioner, right around the time that strangers began to recognize her as that girl in that movie with that guy. Knives come in handy whenever some crazy runs up to you muttering gibberish like, "I loved you in *Ghost Rider*!" **16. A wrap** or vest. A-listers often find themselves on airplanes, jetting off to a sudden change in climate. **17. Body lotion. 18. Magnifying mirror. 19. Hair clips or elastics.** Even if you never use them, carry them. You never know when Angelina Jolie might ambush you at a charity auction and demand that you offer up a personal item for bidding. **20. Press clippings mentioning you.** Some celebrities stash them in their handbags, just to remind themselves why they charge their full appearance fee for a charity gig. Even British actresses have been known to carry their own press clippings, and they're not even really celebrities.

Hair Color Endorsements:

Maintaining Your Hair in the Event of Any Contract

Congratulations on your new home-hair-color endorsement contract. You are, indeed, worth it. And yet, something, some deep and prickly worry, gnaws at you. The vitamin shots and fair-trade soy frappés are no longer keeping you buoyant; you sleep only nine hours a night. This stress is normal for anyone who has just agreed to earn $1 million to $2 million for roughly ten days' work in the hair trade. After all, that money comes with a dark and disturbing price: Your hair—currently bathed in a honey-flaxen incandescence, according to your stylist—will soon come into contact with a product sold at drugstores. These are the same drugstores where large families often purchase emergency supplies of Kraft Macaroni & Cheese

dinner and rectal thermometer covers and lip gloss that is not organic. You fear your hair will never survive an encounter with anything that comes from one of these grimy, back-alley shops.

You may stop worrying immediately. I did some research on this very topic several years ago. In the course of that research, hair colorists told me that, by law, or ethics, or something, the hair color company must apply some measure of its dye to your hair before shooting a commercial for that

The ever-sultry Scarlett Johansson has managed to preserve her trademark blonde locks during her brutal L'Oréal endorsement contract, and so can you.

product—but exactly how much is subject to very creative interpretation.

I was told that decent colorists get around the restrictions by applying the cheap stuff only to the back of a star's head, or maybe just brushing in a few highlights and then treating the rest of the hair with professional-grade color.

Other colorists told me that as little as one strand of your hair must feature the toxic drugstore stuff when you appear in those commercials. In fact, they say, many of the color jobs you see on TV commercials are actually freelance-assigned to outside companies. The feats of cosmetology could be custom jobs using bits of products from other companies, even rivals. In other words, 98 percent of Eva Longoria's burnished-cocoa-bean mane could have been dyed with pigments extracted from centuries-old mahogany bowls once cradled by the hands of a begging Buddha, for all anyone cares. According to those colorists, as long as one strand, or maybe a few locks, of a celebrity spokesmodel's billowing, fan-blown tresses comes from a box of Garnier or Clairol or L'Oréal, it's all good. The rest of your irreplaceable coiffure can remain cocooned in professional-grade products available only in salons.

In the unlikely event that even the professional grade color begins to taint your hair, degrading it from honey-flaxen sunshine into mere spun gold, you can always order the colorists to remove, or dye over, the product immediately after the shoot ends. Top hairstylists say they do that quite often.

There's even more comforting news. Once your commercial shooting ordeal ends, you probably don't ever have to wear that terrifying boxed color ever again, even if your contract has another two years on it. True, some contracts require you to use the products you endorse, but usually not to the exclusion of anything else. As long as you don't disparage your sponsor or heap praise on the competition, you remain generally safe. Page your private hair person immediately and arrange for coif triage.

Fat!

No A-list guide would be complete without reference to fat.

Fat on other people, naturally. Not fat on you, which is ridiculous. Unless you've taken on a brave film role as a tubby serial killer, or some historic monarch in his dropsical gout stage; in that case, *bravisse*. As terrifying as it was for you to invite that loathsome layer of adipose to live inside your body for weeks, remember: It's the fat that can put you over the top for an Oscar nod. Even Zellweger got an Oscar nomination when she porked out for *Bridget Jones's Diary*, and everyone knows that role called for little more than acting hapless and British. Besides, Matt Damon has gotten fat for a role. You really don't need much more comfort than that.[17]

But suppose you awaken one day, looking perhaps a touch jollier than usual. Are you merely Kim Cattrall curvy, or have you gone full Kathleen Turner? Have you eaten and drunk yourself down to the B-list?

Relax. There is an objective criteria set for determining fatness in your business. At times of doubt, simply consult the following minilist:

• The average dress size of an A-list star, according to Hollywood stylists: Zero.

• The average size of a sample garment sent by designers to stars: Two to four.

• The weight of a size-two human being of 5 feet 6 inches or shorter, according to standard clothing catalog guidelines: roughly 105 pounds.

Miley Cyrus has recently embraced a leaner lifestyle. Doctors wonder if her perpetually stuck-out tongue might be a sign of hunger.

[17] **Fine,** so you do need more comfort than that. Very well. Jennifer Hudson won an Oscar *while fat.* That is a verifiable fact.

More 105-pound items:

- The largest cabbage grown in South Central Alaska, according to state records

- The amount of nitrogen recommended to produce 1,500 pounds of cotton on an acre of land

- The healthy weight of a male Labrador retriever

- The estimated amount of marijuana seized by police during a raid in Santa Rosa, California in 2013

- The weight of a hamburger cooked by an ambitious New Jersey man in 2006

See? Easy.

Try on your size-zero jeans. If they no longer fit, you have my permission to panic.

If your size-two dress is also too tight, that means you can no longer squeeze into designer clothes, and your usefulness has officially run out.

You. Are. Fat.

Fighting Fat: A Daily, Low-level Siege

Media reports are rife with tales of marathon celebrity workouts lasting hour after hour. Thank your diabolically mendacious publicist for disseminating this useful urban legend. The truth is, most true A-list stars exercise no more than thirty to forty minutes daily. After all, as an A-lister, you likely have a chef on call—a personal food designer who tracks your daily calorie intake and skillfully redirects your cravings for deep-fried macaroni and cheese balls into more sensible, eggplant-related fare.

Likewise, your frenetic schedule is in a sense an ongoing workout. You tend to leap from project to project, from boutique to spa, from limo to rehab palace, which burns more calories than you can shake a humerus the size of Kate Bosworth at. And as

This wispy little cumulus cloud dresssed up as Keira Knightley for Halloween! Adorbs, right?

you are well aware, the camera lens adds ten Tyra pounds. Consequently, your film career itself requires you to maintain birdlike arms and a clavicle prominent enough to be visible in high-resolution satellite images. With each movie set likely to stock a full array of workout equipment just for you, you probably just haven't had the time to grow fat.

Nonetheless, light daily workouts will keep you toned and camera-ready. A-list workouts require equal parts stealth, stamina, and cunning. You must obtain your cardio and your strength training while simultaneously dodging paparazzi and gawping fans who have paid premium prices to join your elite gym.

Behold, your custom workout, as provided by Nicole Kidman's own Pilates trainer in Los Angeles: Arrive at your spin class or group aerobic workout roughly ten minutes after it begins. You can then work out for a good twenty or twenty-five minutes without suffering too many compliments from adoring fans. Leave the class before it ends and you can avoid that third-class chatter altogether. Now hop in your car and head over to your strength trainer's private studio for another fifteen minutes of toning. You are now free to go. You have completed your exercise regimen for the day. (And, if you are Nicole Kidman, without so much as breaking a sweat on your shiny, pore-free, seemingly cauterized brow.)

That's not sweat on Nicole's disturbingly smooth face; it's a glow.

Drop the String Bean . . . Now! Food and You

Consider your workouts the fun part of celebrity dieting. The other element, the one that your friends never *ever* talk about, is the starvation.

Magazines often trumpet meat-veggie-good-carb celebrity diets that allow about 1,200 calories a day—the minimum intake recommended by responsible health gurus. Much more realistic reports detail 900 calories a day, give or take 100, for an A-list star.[18] If your fridge is stocked with nonfat vanilla yogurt and brown rice, ban those temptations forthwith, or you can start

---

[18] **Actually, scratch that.** A sample menu once released to the media by celebrity trainer Tracy Anderson included eggs and veggie bacon for breakfast; turkey, cucumber, and tomato for lunch; and salmon and Brussels sprouts for dinner. Rough estimate of the total calories, not including drinks, sauces, or other condiments: 683.

slowly and try vegetables. That is, if you want to be a chub like your close friend Victoria Beckham.

Your fellow A-listers have devised a genius method for keeping themselves thin. The approach has an added benefit as well: the ability to tell the press, with a straight face, that they eat whatever they want. The key, as one friend of several A-listers puts it, is "picking"—ordering freely at restaurants, taking one or two bites from a platter, popping an Adderall, and leaving. The method carries the additional benefit of allowing you say—with utter conviction—that you order whatever you like in restaurants.

Of course you can't be expected to remember all this while simultaneously sitting at a restaurant table and drinking water.

Below please find a handy guide to eating macaroni and cheese. Feel free to pop it in your handbag and refer to it in times of doubt.

How to Eat Macaroni and Cheese

Your macaroni and cheese will likely arrive on one large, troughlike platter, making the separation of your portion seem well-nigh impossible. Do not snap at the waitstaff. They may simply be operating on the orders of the chef, who, in turn, might be trying to recreate the barnlike charm of eateries common in other parts of the United States and Canada. Simply request a side plate if one does not arrive automatically.

Place three (3) pieces of macaroni on the side plate. Beware of lurking peas, which contain 117 calories per cup—that's 1.5 calories per pod and .19 calories per pea. Hand the rest of the plate to your lovable little sausage of a size-six assistant. Do your best to refrain from gagging as she momentarily forgets she doesn't live in Fond du Lac anymore and cleans her plate.

Victoria Beckham, looking a bit chunky by Hollywood standards. That's what happens when you binge on lettuce and strawberries.

Eat your three pieces of macaroni, preferably one at a time. If you have worked out today, indulge yourself with a few peas, but make sure your trainer knows about it the next day.

Follow with one Adderall. If anyone should ask, explain that the two-toned blue macaroni you just ate is an elite pasta available only to people who know the chef.

Clenbuterol and Adderall:
Mama's Little *Little* Helpers

Go ahead and walk over to the nearest full-length mirror. If the one directly in front of you isn't getting good light, turn to the one to your left, or right, or whatever one gets decent southern exposure. If you have no full-length mirror in your room, call your moving company to have the item repositioned to your liking immediately.[19]

There. Now, aren't you a pliant young thing? Didn't think pure gold could stand up and walk around, now, did you?

At this point you may notice a centiliter or two of inconvenient fat. This happens to the best of us. If your stylist hasn't got an Adderall or Clenbuterol handy, fire her at once, along with the publicist who referred you to her, and find someone who can supply you with these fabulous, crunchy, slimming treats. These two pills have gained worldwide fame, at least in Los Angeles, for providing quick slim-downs with only the occasional seizure or heart damage.

In the immortal words of the New York *Daily News*, "Female

This is Lindsay Lohan, who totally, TOTALLY doesn't know what you're talking about.

[19] **See page 149** for more information.

celebrities recently arrested—from Paris to Nicole Richie, from Lindsay to Britney Spears —all reportedly have used prescription Adderall. It keeps you awake while killing the appetite." These drugs also have some cute side benefits; Adderall apparently treats attention deficit disorder, and Clen was first developed to help asthma patients—first horse, then human—to breathe better. Paris has said she has ADD. But whether the abovementioned celebrities officially use Adderall for attention deficit, weight loss, or something else entirely also isn't important. What is crucial is this: Lindsay can wear leggings—even metallic space leggings that would make average people resemble Sputnik—and look glorious.

One other note: People who use these drugs for weight loss may face diminishing benefits and eventually start to put on even more unwanted weight, but until then, boy, will you look legendary.

Knowing how to pick just the right tiara was a gift Paris Hilton was born with.

Chop Chop, Fatty:
When Your Skirmishes with Fat Escalate Into An All-Out Hot War

If you have recently had a child, pulled a Christian Bale and gained a bunch of for an Oscar-bait role, or let yourself go in any other way (secret Funion fetish), your trainer may prescribe daily workouts spanning one to two hours until you return to your usual concave, radar-invisible proportions.

Successful techniques for enduring this torture remain few, especially when your towering blond French Adonis of an instructor keeps hovering like a bloodthirsty Luftwaffen Fluglehrer and hitting "repeat" on that electronic mess he picked up in Majorca.

Whatever you do, resist the urge to curse yourself for that sinful romaine-lettuce-and-haddock wrap you scarfed down for breakfast. Simply tell yourself you will *not* abuse your body like that again.

Also refrain from letting your eyes wander to windows or skylights, where curious onlookers can quickly morph into dangerous hallucinations. *Lo, what's this? A strange man, looking in through the ceiling window. Probably just that stalker who keeps calling your houseman over at the Manhattan brownstone. Maybe it's a—what word did Angelina use at her most recent babies shower, some term to describe Third World revolutionaries who perch in trees?—sniper. Yes, perhaps it's a sniper. A mercy killer created from nothing but your Kabbalic prayers and pain, here to relieve you with*

The world quivers on the edge of its seat for even the slightest shift in combined-Kardashian BMI (CKBMI).

Of course Gwyneth named her child Apple. It was the only way she could have one.

one crack shot through this newly discovered portal to freedom. A single, beautiful bullet will remove the grinding agony from your grape-sized calf muscles, forever and ever, and there will be nothing after that, nothing but air and harp music and maybe some fried macaroni and cheese balls with chili fries served up on a big cloud, and—well, now you've blown it. Your nutritionist had warned you that even *visualizing* caloric foods can make you fat. You're lucky if you're not three ounces heavier than when you started.

Never, ever let your mind wander like that. Instead, find a constructive use for your brain. Focus your mind on something fun, such as possible baby names for any children your famous friends may have coming in the future.[20]

[20] **Your friend** Gwyneth already has two kids named Moses Martin and Apple Martin. For the next two kids: Absalom Absalom and Grass. There. Now you try.

CHAPTER THREE

The Press

Getting the Most Out of Your Frenemies

Media is like a knife, or a laser. It can kill, or it can make your face look more fabulous than it's ever looked in your life. Even you, the A-lister, must know how to wield and hone this tool. Your publicist can only ignore so many media calls per week. Inevitably, you will have to face down the press on your own, perhaps after dinner at an intimate, private venue such as the Ivy. This next section tells you everything you need to know.

Try not to malign tabloid reporters too often. Remember that they must wear pants manufactured in large batches in Chinese factories that reek of third-world polymers. They must endure

Lana Del Rey: tries out Pout No. 3 on a red carpet full of test subjects.

the humiliation of yellowish teeth and must type their little stories packed together under fluorescent lights that keep them slow and simple. None of these people have ever felt the creative fire of The Olson Twins from the front row at one of their fashion shows, or had the honor of debating the finer points of *The Secret* with Oprah.

If you must speak to a reporter directly, show patience. Yes, *at one time*, you were more than happy to share your kinky turn-ons with *Cosmo*, or pose in a thong for *Stuff*, or participate in staged "romantic getaways" with your very-not-gay costars while pre-approved paparazzi "hounded" you from their "hiding place" in the "bushes."

But that was before you made the A-list. You are now a public figure, which makes you a very private person. Questions about who you're dating are way, way too personal. Of course that concept isn't really that hard for people at your level to understand. Show restraint: This sad, gritty world is counting on you to keep it bright. Be strong, for the sake of this benighted planet.

Publicists: Sometimes Feral, Always Necessary

Your publicist serves as a gateway between you and the estimated six billion other people on the planet, with the notable exception of the Dalai Lama, who can, and does, call your house direct whenever he wants. At roughly $3,000 to $8,000 per month, a personal publicist may seem like an unnecessary expense, especially when a movie studio publicist, manager, agent, or attorney can ignore the press's phone calls as well as anyone from BWR.

You may also wonder whether you can trust your publicist to understand your needs. After all, it's not she who must

Watching your publicist choose her strategy is a little like watching a flashdance. Never, ever stifle her creative vision.

There's a reason why so many Oscar winners thank their publicists. Their publicists are the ones approving their outfits. For the Oscars. Really.

have *her* teeth brushed and *her* yoga pants on by 6 AM so that she can be driven to the movie set. And it's not she who must endure those lukewarm fair-trade soy-chai lattes—how many times must you indicate *extra hot?*—during that endless, endless ride.

Yes, your publicist grew up in Calabasas, so she has known a kind of character-building pain. But really. Publicity falls under the category of "practice," but acting falls under the rubric of "art" (or in the case of television, "craft") and requires real suffering to do well. Consider the emotional turmoil you endure every time you conjure tears on the set, often as part of the scene you are in. Your publicist has never truly suffered, not even that time you made her issue the press release while having her lower intestine removed. Even counting that, she isn't anywhere *·near* in touch with the kind of inner torment you simulate every day of your life.

★★★★**A-List Tip**

Transforming Press Photographers into Personal Portraitists

Does your new baby need its first passport photo? Is a photographer from *OK!* or *Vogue* coming to your home to interview you and take a few snapshots? Are you getting the "picture"? Your fellow A-listers routinely ask professional shutterbugs—a potential wedding photographer, in one instance—to take their baby's first passport photo while they're on the job. Killing two birds with one shoot: It just makes sense.

Why hire a publicist, also known as, in the words of Hollywood's more delightfully decrepit citizenry, a press agent—apart from the fact that she'll plan every single one of your weddings for free?

Because not every crisis in life is large. Sometimes you get a whole bunch of mini-crises that glom together and, if left untreated, can form a giant megacrisis. (To answer the question in your head right now: Yes, the giant crisis usually does have the exact same shape and proportions as the tiny crises, but on a massive scale—just like a giant fly that's made up of tiny flies.) And during those times, it's best to have someone else standing by to not return the media's calls.

Specifically,

your publicist can and *should*:

- **Dictate exactly which amazing** photo of you will grace the cover of a monthly magazine. Every major publicist does this or, at least, tries to get away with doing this. Demanding final approval of your cover photos may trigger complaints from editors about "quashing journalistic freedom," but, really. Anyone who uses "quashing" in a sentence is a tool.

- **Blacklist reporters who** ask you daunting questions, or dare to write so-called "balanced"[21] things about you,[22] or print information about your personal life without sharing the profits from such disclosures. Again, most power publicists do this in their sleep.

- **Order—not request—**reporters to avoid entire topics[23] and even specific words[24] or phrases during interviews. If you still fear that a reporter may ask a question that will confuse or in any way stimulate you, just do what Angelina Jolie once did: Force all reporters to sign legal documents outlining precisely what they can and cannot ask.

- **Get on the blower.** Publicists love to breathe napalm at reporters through their little Bluetooth headsets. Sometimes they threaten lawsuits. Other times they prefer to declare: "None. Of my clients. Will ever. Speak to you. Again."

---

[21] **BAL-inst:** Meanness disguised as "facts" about you, such as your height, or your hometown.

[22] A publicist working with Tobey Maguire once did that, banning *Us Weekly* from a red-carpet movie premiere of his after they published some unauthorized something or other. And Tobey isn't really an A-lister anymore. Not even when there's an old *Spider-Man* movie on TV.

[23] During one press junket, Guy Ritchie's publicist commanded reporters to avoid all Madonna-related queries. A writer who asked about son Rocco was dismissed.

[24] Before a writer for London's *Guardian* could interview pouty French actress Emmanuelle Béart, a handler reportedly banned any questions containing the words "lips" or "collagen."

Emergency Scenario:
You Get a Qualm

You may occasionally suffer a pang of guilt over hiring your toddler-chewing harpy of a press agent. Kill that pang immediately. Just because she fantasizes about filing her teeth into sharp points does not mean that your publicist is inherently evil. Nor does the fact that staring directly at the First Amendment can singe her flesh and melt her eyes, or that she occasionally uses her connections with you to burnish her own image,[25] or that she tends to treat reporters like employees.[26] Everyone should be allowed their individual weaknesses.

Your publicist is your ambassador to the rest of the world. Which explains her awesome people skills.

---

[25] A publicist for **Jennifer Lopez** once successfully killed an accurately reported article—not because of what the story said about her client, but because of what it said about her.

[26] Even the publicists for the Oscars, who represent no celebrity in particular, require reporters to cover the Academy Award nominations before they can get credentials for the final ceremony.

Fighting Back
Against Press Attack

At some point the press is likely to realize your importance to the world community and attempt a character assassination. These reporters will stop at nothing to crush your painstakingly developed public persona, shielding themselves under some made-up aegis of "balanced reporting" or "the First Amendment." They may assert, via photo spread or words, that you are "just like"

Kristen Stewart's publicist forgot to tell her not to make out with married guys in public places. Bad publicist! Bad!

them in some way. (Telling people that you're just like everyone else is, of course, *your* job, to be recited during press junkets at the Four Seasons. Having a strange writer say that makes it false, of course, unless that writer is your good friend Joel Coen.)

Some writer may also try to "blow the lid off" how you got that amazing glow on the Oscars red carpet. (It was, of course, your natural radiance, which you get every time you run after one of your beautiful children. It was not "bronzer," as your makeup artist was quoted as saying. But these magazines never want the *truth*, which your poor publicist spent hours and hours crafting just for your fans.)

Pressback Tactics:

Here is how real movie stars—just like you!—put rogue reporters on a leash:

1. Six Degrees of Blackballing, OR, How to Leverage Your Tenuous Connection with Another A-Lister to Kill Any Magazine Story on Earth

Before you shell out for a publicist, ask your assistant to go to the Web site www.WhoRepresents.com. (The site charges a monthly fee to join, but it's nothing your assistant can't afford.)

The site lists the agents, lawyers, and publicists for almost every star who has one. It also works backward, listing every talent represented by a certain lawyer, agent, or publicist. Your assistant should click on your probable publicist's name and see a list of every other famous person he or she represents.

Ignore the smaller names, like those unfortunate cast members from that rock-and-roll forensics show. Instead look for names at your level—Tom Cruise, perhaps, or a member of the British royal family. The publicist who represents them really should represent you. You may never have met these actors, but they are now your very good friends, and not just because you say that in interviews. They are about to save you from the feckless mob in the Chinese pants. And one day, when some lithe young man emerges from a public sauna in Tarzana claiming he knows the exact size of

Angelina Jolie

Paris Hilton poses with her best friend.

Tom Cruise's Thetans, you, through your publicist, will save Tom right back.

A good publicist can threaten media outlets with a blackball treatment: run a negative story about one of the publicist's clients and lose access to every other A-list client on her list, forever and in perpetuity.

This threat happens to at least one news outlet a week from some A-list publicist, and that's because it works. To be fair, everyone wins. The mean story gets killed. You and your fellow A-listers continue to forge your unique spiritual bond. The reporter gets the reassurance that someone close to the A-listers is actually paying attention, which is the whole reason the writers got into this business in the first place.

2. Being Your Own Best Friend, OR How to Plant Quotes While Maintaining Plausible Deniability (aka the "Paris Hilton Method")

There may come a day when you have to initiate direct contact with a reporter. (Let's say your publicist gets uppity and turns off her phone while she's lollygagging in the emergency room. You may have to fire her, but, for the moment, there is no need to fear.) There is, in fact, a very safe method of doing this, one that requires no touching and has produced strong results for tabloid fixtures. I cannot tell you exactly which fixtures, because, of course, Paris Hilton is an extremely private person.

"The Paris Hilton Method"

Step ONE

Obtain the cell phone number—not office, not home—of a tabloid reporter.

Step TWO

Send a text message to that reporter saying that you will feed him *incredible true information* about *yourself* starting *right now.*

Step THREE

You may hear only silence for the next several hours, as the reporter informs the necessary editors, treats the stain on his pants, and grows accustomed to his newly elevated rank among the various reporting clans.

Step FOUR

Explain that you have two conditions: 1) You are only to be quoted as an anonymous "friend" of yourself. and 2) you have the right to text the reporter whenever you want and instruct him to kill any story about you that you don't like.

Step FIVE

Feel your new power. Continue to text the reporter as often as you like—several times a night, if you wish. Regale your new writer-slash-assistant with fresh, riveting quotes, all culled from your stunning performance as your mysterious, jet-setting—but not quite so beautiful—best friend. Where this tabloid is concerned, you will always and forever remain the anonymous friend of yourself. If you fear a clever observer may eventually figure out that you and your "friend" are one and the same, you can always switch tactics rechristen yourself "a source close to the star."

Any reporter who refuses to cooperate is probably suffering under the strain of some sort of "journalism school" or "ethics training" and should be discarded immediately. Simply get your assistant to find another cell number and try again. Of course you could instruct your assistant or publicist to try steps 1 through 3 on your behalf. It is also acceptable for a star—even one of your caliber—to handle it personally. Plenty of other celebrities have done this, including, according to my own sources, Lindsay Lohan and Denise Richards.

The next time a rival celeb pisses you off, go ahead and feed something mean about her to your new assistant in the media. Other stars do. All the time. Via their anonymous, if not real, close friends.

3. Just Call the Paparazzi, Already

Many, many celebrities, including Kim Kardashian, Paris Hilton, Kathy Griffin, David Duchovny, and even A-listers like you, reportedly have staged photo ops for the paparazzi, or tipped paps off to their own where abouts when the need arose. These A-Listers:

- Personally call the photographers.
- Cooperate at the behest of a publicity-seeking director or PR maven.
- Instruct their publicists to call the paps.
- Inform a friendly magazine editor that they, say, will be at such-and-such a park between, say, noon and 1 PM, frolicking with their child in bare feet and perhaps a lovely skirt, and looking like an excellent mother, and if a paparazzo would like to be lurking in the bushes of his own accord, trying to capture that bond in film, neither man nor Spielberg will interfere.

Kim Kardashian, professional poseur.

If you try this last tactic, be sure to choose a quiet place with plenty of bushes where the paparazzi can hide. Paparazzi work largely at night, seeking the shelter of small, enclosed, dark spaces while waiting for celebrities to appear; they may grow disoriented or emit sizzling noises and puffs of smoke when exposed to sun.[27]

Don't worry about your contact with paparazzi getting out into the press. Most paparazzi are way too busy insulting each other in exotic accents to expose you. Besides, like most people, they would much rather be your friend.

---

[27] **Or just puffs** of cigarette smoke.

Developing Your
Storybook Romance
Weddings For Fun and Profit

We are living in a dark time. In days past, French peasants would dress in gaily torn rag ensembles and steal glimpses of glorious royal weddings; England's Henry VIII staged elaborate plays for his lucky wives and subjects, with him as the star; and Stalin produced riveting show trials for the benefit of his people, who thanked him by acting scared. In the twenty-first century, we have no autocrats to dazzle the citizenry and keep them from rioting or accidentally eating ergot-infected bread. It's all up to you, and the planners of your wedding, to maintain that delicate peace.

There's no use pretending it won't be stressful for you. You'll probably have to check in with your publicist at least once a week to see how the planning is going. You also must deliver a draining real-life performance, denying your engagement, and denying and denying, until the very day of the wedding.[28] And of course someone will have to come up with a decent fake name under which you can file your bridal registry.

But you can, and will, get through it—probably at least twice. Remember: Weddings can also prove equally fun and cheap for a major star.

Just a few short years ago, an A-lister could actually make a profit off of a wedding by selling exclusive photos. Your darling buds Catherine Zeta Jones and Michael Douglas got a reported $1.4 million from OK! magazine for their wedding pics. Eva Longoria reportedly scored $2 million for hers. Nowadays, such deals are increasingly rare, unless you happen to have a name that rhymes with, say, Yangelina Folie. That's the bad news. The good news: You can still leverage your fame to get a six-figure nuptial party at a fraction of the price.

Johnny Depp has announced plans to marry longtime partner: his fedora, Phillip. Oh, sorry I mean: his girlfriend, Amber Heard.

[28] **Such a tactic** is reserved for serious A-listers only. If you fear that you might be slipping down into the B-list, Instagram a photo of your engagement ring immediately upon acceptance. At least one TV sitcom star has gained a whole new audience by simply getting engaged and letting the world know about it.

Here's how: Once you acquire your engagement diamond—that small moon orbiting beautifully around your left ring finger—have your publicist contact a fancy magazine, such as Martha Stewart Weddings, or Vogue. Your publicist will then offer that magazine exclusive behind-the-scenes access to your big day. In exchange, the magazine will essentially plan your wedding for you. They will use their clout to help you acquire the fanciest flowers, the most ethereal linens, and yummiest cake you could ever pretend to eat, and all at a deep, deep discount.[29] As one celebrity wedding planner put it to me, you're essentially getting the best editorial stylists on Earth—people who otherwise just don't do weddings—and they're going to make everything look fabulous, to boot.

[29] **Just how deep?** Well, write down your wedding budget, which, if you're a true A-lister, will run between $500,000 to $2 million. Then subtract 60 to 70 percent.

Shopping While
Famous: Acquiring the Perfect Diamond Engagement Ring

Your publicity lockdown should start as soon as the ring seeker strikes out to find a large diamond not yet acquired by Jennifer Lopez. By striking out, I mean out of the bedroom

---

Emergency Scenario:

Only One Half of Your Celebrity Couple Is Famous, and It Isn't the Half Buying the Ring

Do not waste precious hours attempting to visit Julia Roberts to seek advice. Yes, she married that guy, Anonymous Q. Whatshisname, so she has the relevant experience to help you. But then again, Julia often ensconces herself deep inside her Taos ranch, surrounded by fried-up locals so sun-baked and delusional they may mistake you for a Comanche and shoot on sight. Instead, resist the urge to go anywhere at all. Suppose for a second, in some alternate universe, that your husband-to-be isn't just an unknown but a complete nobody—say, a ditch-digger at Macy's. Even then, because of *your* major star status,

diamond industry representatives say he can score a serious discount on the 5-carat, heart-shaped canary diamond you've had your eye on: The one with the 4.5-karat ventricle-shaped pink diamond encrusted inside. There. You may cease to panic.

---

or home office and into the living room, where privileged jewelers are standing by to present their creations with trembling hands. A-list celebrities rarely leave their homes to shop for major items; even cars are purchased with a single phone call to a dealer, who then does his best to suppress his rapturous tremors while delivering the vehicle to a star's home.

If the ring seeker must leave his home or office to shop for your engagement ring, either he's not famous enough, or you aren't. In either case, fire your publicist.

Also fire your publicist if your fiancé cannot secure a proper discount on the ring. Diamond industry insiders have estimated to me that A-listers have enjoyed ring discounts as deep as 50 to 75 percent. Which means, for you, 75 percent. So let's just say, in some bizarro alternate universe, your fiancé wanted to buy you a tiny, 1-carat blue diamond

Emergency Scenario:

Jennifer Lopez Wants Your Diamond

Ignore any mutual friends who insist she can smell fear. There is nothing doglike about Jennifer Lopez; she fits more easily into the avian category, given her crowlike affinity for fixing upon shiny objects, even from a great height. Little is known about her running speed, though her preference for T-strap heels cannot work in her favor. If directly confronted, do not back down, but do not make direct eye contact, either. Eventually a paparazzo flashbulb will erupt, momentarily blinding Lopez and affording you a few seconds to take flight.

Jennifer Lopez

inside a wee wad of platinum, you know, as a joke. If that toy ring retailed for $150,000, your fiancé might pay no more than $37,500. In other words, about what you'd throw down for your everyday Hermes alligator-skin handbag.

Your Priceless Wedding Gown, and How Not To Pay For It

For years, you have made millions of people laugh and cry. In return, other than your standard eight-figure fee and absolute embargo on eye contact, you ask for so little. No wonder so many top fashion labels want to give you a wedding gown for free.

However, there's something you should know. Those labels are lowballing you. They're cheating you. *They're insulting you.* Because, these days, A-list actresses don't just get their wedding gowns for free. They charge for the privilege. Let me restate that just in case your assistant didn't get it: *True megastars not only get their wedding gowns for free. They also require a payout from fashion labels for the exclusive use of their bodies on their wedding day.* On at least two recent occasions, fashion labels have even gotten into bidding wars over who gets to dress an A-list bride.

```
            A-LIST PLAYBOOK
          YOUR WEDDING BUDGET
              MADE SIMPLE

225/2653/019283 DN 1PC 3/4 PRNT DRS

UPC NO. 877236536786
STARTING FIGURE FOR AN A-LIST WEDDING
          QTY 1     1,000,000.00
  NET SALES/RETURN VALUE       0.00

UPC NO. 657126885036
AVERAGE MAGAZINE OPENING BID FOR A-LIST
WEDDING PHOTOS
          QTY 1 1,000,000.00
NET SALES/RETURN VALUE         0.00

UPC NO. 657126844094
ADDITIONAL WEDDING PHOTO FEE (BECAUSE
YOU ARE NEITHER ASHLEE OR EVA)
          QTY 1 2,000,000.00
NET SALES/RETURN VALUE         0.00

******************************************
          SUBTOTAL 4,000,000.00
NON TAXABLE 0.0000% 15205      0.00
SALES TAX 7.0000% 15205 280,000.00
          TOTAL 4,280,000.00

     TOTAL ITEMS SOLD: 3
   TOTAL ITEMS RETURNED: 0
  ALL SALES ARE FINAL/NO RETURNS

 TRIPLE PLATINUM VISA-4,280,000.00
XXXXXX7654/XXXX/00986783M

  REMAINING BALANCE          0.00

  ACCOUNT CREDIT (A-LIST PERK
  FOR USING YOUR VISA CARD)
                   2,000,000.00
SO WHY NOT RESERVE VERSAILLES PALACE
FOR THE RECEPTION?
```

Preserving Your Wedding's ~~Dollar Value~~ Privacy

Your publicist should be well aware of the array of dangers that threaten the security of your fabulous wedding. In the interest of caution, you should also acquaint yourself with these hazards, in case your publicist is too busy being one of your bridesmaids to be much of an employee.

Hazard 1 Your Office of Vital Records, An Insidious Spy Network Financed by Public Dollars

Your privacy is much more important than that of an unfamous person. (Your publicist can confirm this for you, at any time, night or day. Don't be afraid to call and ask often.) And yet, marriages, births, and deaths remain a matter of public record. For everyone—including you. Anyone—people who own fewer than three Birkin handbags—can skulk into a local hall of records and find out whether you're alive—*without having to call your publicist first.*

It's an outrage. You have done more than enough for America by sharing your baked ziti recipe with Oprah and airing those priceless revelations about your co-star's on-set pranks. (Clooney: Such a card!)

No one can defeat this cruel, misguided law, but your fellow A-listers have perfected three arcane tactics aimed at thwarting the process, or, at least, slowing it down.

Solution 1: **HOUSE CALLS**

When two unfamous people wish to marry, they must go to their city hall and apply for a marriage license—usually at least one day before the ceremony. Local officials do not make house calls for this breed of person.[30] But they do make them for you. Late on the night of July 3, 2002, just minutes before Julia Roberts married that workaday camera slinger, she summoned a county clerk to the Taos compound to issue a last-minute marriage license. The result: Knowledge of her wedding was sealed in a protective cocoon of secrecy for roughly six hours. And the clerk, of course, now has a cherished memory of meeting Julia Roberts. Such a process is a win-win for all. Do not get married without arranging for this house call. If the registrar balks at the inconvenience of it all, offer him or her something priceless, such as a photo of the two of you together during the historic notarization. Be sure to have the photo laminated; otherwise it is likely to be lovingly stroked to death.

Solution 2: **CREATIVE FABRICATION**

Never underestimate the value of a good liar. Caterers, event designers, venue operators—the creativity of their fibs is just as important as the originality of their lamb crostini. Any top-quality wedding vendor will lie on your behalf without being asked. In June 2003, the event liaison of the Museum of Asian Art was telling future brides that her venue didn't do weddings. Christy Turlington's wedding reception was hosted there that same month.

Solution 3: **FAKE WEDDINGS**

A mere piece of paper cannot possibly represent or contain the legendary love that you feel for your next spouse-to-be. Yours is a romance writ large, larger even than the IMAX format. For you and the conjugal accessory, a marriage license is a mere token, and one that is largely irrelevant. What's more, legal recognition of your joyous *People* magazine cover-to-be may not be worth the invasion of your precious privacy that ensues whenever you file a so-called "public" document. For you there is an alternative to a wedding license. Simply stage a ceremony that *looks* like a wedding and you'll have no need to file any public records whatsoever. Eddie Murphy and Brandy have staged less-than-official ceremonies that looked like weddings, but had no official sanction "in the eyes of the state." If you want your wedding to be legit in a legal sense, you will eventually have to file for a marriage license, but at least your formal ceremony will have gone forward unsullied.

---

[30] **Citizens** of common stock can hire a service that will let them file the wedding paperwork from the comfort of their living units. Of course, unlike you, who offers so much to the world unbidden, they have to pay for it.

Hazard 2 Air

Don't forget to reserve the airspace above your wedding venue before the big day. Ditto with the roads. Your privacy is much more important than taxpayer access to public freeways on a weekend near a major beach. Your fellow A-listers occasionally practice this simple principle. In 2000, Brad Pitt shut down part of the Pacific Coast Highway (California State Route 1), which connects Southern Californians to several miles of public beaches, on the Saturday of his now-defunct wedding to Jennifer Aniston. Law enforcement officers also banned beachgoers seeking parking spaces within several blocks of the event. The Federal Aviation Administration even shut down the airspace over the Malibu estate hosting the wedding, to make sure no media choppers encroached on the sacred day. There. Doesn't it feel better to know your rights?

Solution:

IF YOUR VENDOR cannot secure the airspace around your event, you have an alternative—one that celebrity wedding planners occasionally use. Rent a venue with a helipad on it. FAA regulations require a minimum space between all running helicopters, airborne or not. Pay a little pilot man—an "admiral," or "leftenant," or whatever they go by—to sit in a helicopter with the motor running—and maybe, just for fun, with the whirlygig thing turning. As long as the engine is turned on, no other helicopter can fly near the area. And that, of course, includes choppers carrying paparazzi.

**Don't Forget
to Regift
Something
Nice for Your
Publicist**

Most A-list
weddings are
spearheaded primarily
by the stars' publicists.
The publicists or
assistants. screen
wedding vendors,
arrange security,
consult on guest
lists, and haggle
with media over
photo sales. The
next time you
get a voucher for
free Restylane
injections, pass
them on to your
publicist as a
thank-you for
her free wedding
consultations.
You can't smooth
out her pinched
personality, but
you can offer to
chemically banish
those Robert Blake
marionette lines.

Hazards 3 & 4
Joy and Other People

Beware of joy. It can make you soft and weak, vulnerable to myriad plots and hostile intrigue. Even during your most sacred and special day, surrounded by squadrons of ex-Mossad security lugs, you are never safe from the prying eyes of adoring fans. Whether you are getting married in a church, at a resort, in a producer's mansion, on a private island, or behind the barricades of your own compound, paparazzi can and will find ways to photograph you looking gorgeous on terms that are not entirely under your control. Nothing is more horrifying than looking beautiful and not having the correct lighting to showcase it properly.[31]

Even if you avoid unauthorized photos, there are other, perhaps even more disturbing, perils. Strange people might discover the color of your wedding bouquet, or the flavor of the cake you served, and talk about it without previous authorization from your camp. This is absolutely unacceptable, of course. Even after your wedding is long over, an exclusive event loses a little bit of its "specialness" every time an unfamous person learns a new detail about it. Everyone knows that. By the time two million nonindustry people have read that you used grapefruit-sized peonies supplied by Stanlee Gatti, your wedding has been completely devalued and you may as well start over and plan another one.

Very often, paparazzi and reporters achieve their nefarious goals by paying off neighbors or caretakers of nearby buildings. In exchange for these bribes, the press receives a bird's-eye view, postevent details, or both. Very little can be done to stave off this unimaginable nightmare.[32]

---

[31] With the possible exception of looking beautiful on a magazine cover that you were not paid to pose for.

[32] **As of publication time**, no A-lister has attempted to invoke the right of eminent domain over venue-adjacent private property. However, your lawyers might want to look into relevant legal precedents, possibly in pre–Magna Carta court documents.

Solution:

APPROACH YOUR neighbors before the press can. Better yet, have your assistant, publicist, or ex-Mossad security goon approach the neighbors. Make sure your operative is armed with a large wad of cash. Offer to pay the neighbors a "rental fee" for the exclusive "use" of their property or balcony for the duration of your "birthday party." Failure to do this will result in the press swooping in later, harpy-like, or perhaps in the manner of flying monkeys, to offer similar bribes. (Paparazzi photographing the Stefani wedding in London got a crow's-nest view of the church court-yard by infiltrating a nearby building.)

If you can stand it, consider inviting these neighbor folk to your ceremony.[33] If they feel included in the elite event, they are less likely to blab about it later (especially under a binding nondisclosure agreement), and they certainly won't be at home, where they are vulnerable to press bribes.

If all else fails, you can do what an increasing number of stars are doing: Book a wedding at a giant resort or some other estate, and rent out every single room in the place, whether they're going to use it or not. Paparazzi banned. Problem solved.

Gavin Rossdale is pictured here with his wife, the most lucrative feather duster on Earth. Her wedding dress was custom-made by John Galliano, who was on hand the entire time, just in case something unfashionable were to happen at the last minute.

---

[33] **Inviting such folk**, while unimaginably generous, does not fall under the category of charity and cannot be written off on your yearly tax filing. Budget accordingly.

Emergency Scenario:

Bride and Groom Are Living Legends

Time for an Operation Double-A Wedding.

In the event of a star-on-star wedding (legal in many states), media interest in every detail will escalate to *Sex and the City* reunion–proportion. You'll need to at least quadruple your secrecy measures. A double A-lister wedding often in-

Not married. Not yet. Hold on. Checking. Nope. Still not.

volves a level of intrigue worthy of James Bond. The new, hot James Bond, of course, not the really old one with the hairy-eyebrow condition.

What follows is a short overview of the typical superstar-on-superstar wedding, based on the experiences of your fellow actual A-listers who have paved the way in recent years.

• **All wedding details will be** screened through a publicist or assistant. Hundreds of workers will converge to make your wedding the most personal and intimate it can be. Fortunately, you will never have to meet most of them.

• **Wedding vendors will not** be told who the client is until the day of the wedding. Some vendors, such as florists, often aren't told at all. Instead they usually enjoy a delightful surprise the following month, when they get the new issue of *InStyle* and see their cream orchid arrangements cradled in your one-of-a-kind hands.

- **Your wedding-gown-** designer-slash-very-good-friend—say, Carolina Herrera—shall be told to make you a diamond-white, floor-length gown with a thirty-foot train and matching veil for you to wear to "mom's anniversary party." (Even as Herrera went about the feverish business of fitting her friend Renée Zellweger for a long white gown, she was never told it was for the actress's now-defunct marriage to Kenny Chesney. Being a properly submissive friend, Herrera never asked. "I didn't want to ask too much," Herrera later told *Women's Wear Daily*.)

- **Wedding vendors shall** never, ever be told the exact day of your wedding until a week before the event. Instead, your publicist will instruct the vendors to hold a window of dates free. A ten-day window around Thanksgiving usually works fine. The vendors will gladly sacrifice those thousands of dollars in business and the time with their families just for the chance to come within fifty feet of your publicist.

- **Vendors will not learn the** exact location of your nuptials until the morning of your vows. Neither will your guests, in fact. Instead, guests will be told what to pack ahead of the event, and how many days they should block out. The precise longitude and latitude of the nuptials will not be known unto them until their private plane touches down.

- **Your security team will** frisk everybody as they enter the wedding venue. Really. Everybody. Frisk your mom. Frisk your aunt. Pat down all the guests, even your buddy Jay-Z, who tends to show up at weddings with his own two-man bodyguard team. Make sure none of 'em have cell phones. Because cell phones have cameras. And cameras take pictures. And the only people who are supposed to be taking pictures are your friends at *Vogue*, remember?

- **And of course, all vendors** should be required to sign a nondisclosure agreement. These binding contracts ensure that you, you alone, can sell the exclusive details of your wedding to the highest-bidding magazine without hindrance.[34]

---

[34] **Make sure your** NDAs have teeth. For a typical A-list wedding, the NDA stipulates that, if a vendor blabs without permission, the bride and groom can sue that business for $5 million for breach of privacy.

CHAPTER FIVE

Children and Other Personal Projects

For you, the A-list actress, there is no wrong time to get pregnant. The world has wanted you to spin off a nugget of your 24-karat DNA—which is, for the record, an American treasure—ever since you broke big. Having a baby is an excellent way to show the world exactly how selfless you are; after all, in reproducing, you will provide an echo of your own likeness, a scion who can shine a (slightly dimmer) headlamp of excellence long after you have passed on. Having a family also has direct benefits for you, the A-list parent. As an investment, a family will pay big dividends for years to come. Literally. The baby photos alone can win you millions of dollars. Invest that cash wisely and you can pull in an extra five figures yearly, just from interest. If you ever face a media attack accusing you of less-than-stellar morals, you can negate it by leaking a squishy, taffy-coated story about your family ski vacation to a national magazine in a matter of minutes.

In birthing a child, you will doubtlessly embark on your most personal project to date, not including that incredible bit of magical realism you cocreated with your dear friend Baz Luhrmann.[35] Fight the temptation to over-plan your pregnancies. Jessica Alba recently suffered a serious case of unexpected pregnantitis, and instead of stalling her career, it earned her enough positive ink to nearly erase public memory of those *Fantastic Four* movies.

Instead, focus less on the *timing* of the birth, and more on the *marketing* of said birth. Jennifer Lopez reportedly fetched $4 million to $6 million for exclusive first photos of her twins—not bad, given that her latest reported asking price for a movie was $12 million. Christina Aguilera squeezed a reported $2 million to $3 million out of *People* magazine for the first photos of her son. Even Jamie Lynn Spears, whose star wattage falls somewhere between phosphorescing fungi and a stick-up bulb, extracted a reported $1 million from another magazine for photos of her baby.

Nowadays, magazines just don't pay that much. But you can still use your baby to enhance your brand as a glamorous "working mom." Fire up that Instagram account and fill it with photos of you and your baby on the road. They'll keep you famous even if you don't have, say, an album dropping that week.[36]

Whether you decide you want to sell your

---

[35] **If you don't** have a womb, feel free to skip this section.

[36] **Hi,** Beyonce! Give my best to Blue Ivy.

baby photos or not, your pregnancy is definitely a chance to boost your star power. Once your publicist confirms the pregnancy to *People* magazine (on the record) and to *US Weekly* (off the record) the whole world will rejoice with you. Your dear friends at Prada and Gucci will stay up for three nights straight, designing custom baby hats and wraps and blankets made from mink pups and fetal-stage chinchilla. Nursery decorators will slash their prices—or even eliminate them altogether—just

Jessica Alba. Look at her. Don't you just want to pelt her with gifts? Really, really hard?

for the honor of providing your baby with its first Bel Bambini mobile. Your very own international bumpwatch will engross the entire planet for months. Once you do get pregnant, be sure to congratulate yourself. You've just given the entire world something to celebrate.

Debuting a Child the A-list Way:
Via Cesarean

Your child, as yet unborn and therefore still in development, nonetheless has already captivated the world, much like an excellent teaser trailer. You wouldn't open your next blockbuster in a seedy second-run art house, so there's no reason to premiere your most precious sequel (the baby) in a manner less than befitting an A-lister, which means natural childbirth is *out of the question.*

Sadly, in less fortunate parts of the world and indeed in many of the United States, women reportedly still deliver newborns *through their genitals.*[37] This often takes place in rooms with no private kitchens or flat-screen TVs. Now, there may in fact be charities working selflessly to end the primitive and barbaric scourge of birth-canal birth. I *personally* don't know of any such charities because, thankfully, they have not recently shut down the streets in my neighborhood for one of their "walks," making it impossible for me to drive *anywhere* to get a latte. However, I do know this: It is a tragic but very real fact that in the twenty-first century, many women in the so-called first world continue to suffer the disfiguring stigma of natural childbirth.

Yes. I said disfiguring. Which is why you, A-lister, want and need a cesarean section.

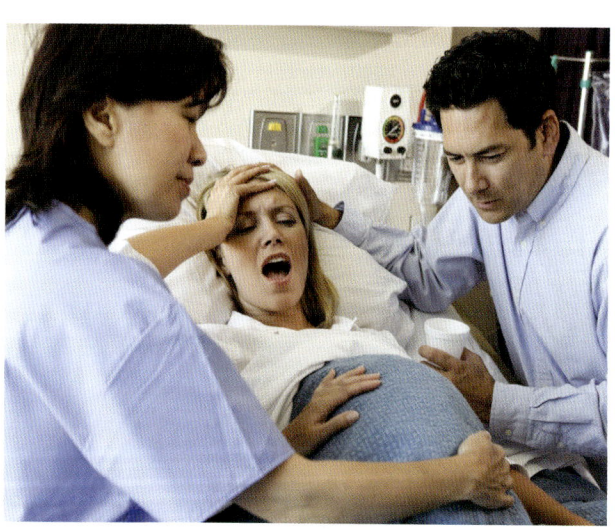

This unfortunate woman, possibly of Midwestern stock, must deliver her child through her genitals.

Pushing could result in unforeseen cosmetic disaster. People outside your industry—milkmaids, perhaps—do not need to worry about maybe popping a blood vessel that could later show up in one of those double-page spreads in *US Weekly* or *Life & Style*—the ones with the cruel yellow circles drawn

---

[07] **yes.** True.

around poor Beyoncé's back fat.

I said "disfiguring" a few sentences ago in order to get your attention. (It worked like a charm!) Potential physical trauma isn't even the biggest of the child-bearing A-lister's concerns. In fact, the main reason why most celebrities adore C-sections is because a controlled medical procedure allows them to plan the delivery down nearly to the second. In fact you (meaning your assistant) can schedule the exact date of your cesarean months in advance. Until biotechnology advances to the point where fetuses become iPhone-proficient (all of the posher geneticists are currently working on this), a C-section ensures that your child will arrive promptly at the time most convenient for you and your

Shakira's hips did not lie—about being too small to squeeze out her massive baby boy, Milan.

Kate Hudson: proud member of The C-Club.

shooting schedule. For example, you can take a cue from Denise Richards, who said she booked her cesarean delivery to fall within her then-husband's TV sitcom hiatus. Unfortunately the baby didn't get the memo and arrived a day early. Then again, Denise Richards is a C-lister. You are so not. Your baby wouldn't dare risk the wrath of your agents at CAA and arrive at any time other than the right time.[38]

If none of the above intelligence has convinced you of your need for a C-section, then fine. Here come the big guns: Madonna and Jolie have both had them. So as you can see, there is nothing particularly C-list about C-sections (Tori Spelling and Denise Richards notwithstanding).

---

[38] **Also,** please consider your lackeys at the tabloids. Tori Spelling scheduled the C-section for her daughter, Stella, for a Monday. *OK!* magazine's deadline is Monday night. Probably a coincidence. But certainly a happy one for the scribes at *OK!*

Emergency Scenario:

Your OB-GYN Is Yammering Something About the Risks of a C-section

Tell the busybody quack that your Pilates-taut abdominal muscle walls may not be able to sustain a natural birth. No kidding. You aren't making this up. Some very real birthing nurses have told me that if a patient is *too toned*, her baby cannot properly flip upside down into the birth position. This, apart from being nature's way of complimenting you on your hot abs, can be a potentially life-threatening situation. If Dr. "Ethics" paid attention in med school, she'll realize that a C-section is the only option for you.

The look that Madonna uses whenever she requests a C-section.

Receiving Tribute For Your Child:
Why You Need a Baby Registry

You may not think you need a baby registry or even a shower, given that you alone could buy every fleece blanket that passes through the Petit Tresor boutique until the sun fades into a white dwarf. But many other people need your baby shower. Let your friends in the retail and entertainment industry thank you for leaving a bit of yourself for the next generation. They really do want to. Don't you, yourself, sometimes feel like throwing gifts at adorable people, like Jessica Alba—Jessica, with her juicy jellybean of an upper lip, and her big, soft, chocolate-brown eyes, and a smile the likes of which America hasn't seen since Barbie introduced her sassy sister Skipper back in '64? Now you can understand the people who want to throw you a shower. If they could throw you a shower every day, just for being you, they would.

So many people want to thank you for reproducing. For Lord's sake, let them.

The fact is that you'll likely experience an average of three baby showers before your resplendent DNA nugget arrives. Alba sure did—including one thrown by Tyra Banks on her now defunct TV show—and Alba, as of press time, still wasn't an official member of the A-list.

Also consider using your baby registry to show the world how humble you have become since you learned of your pregnancy. Leave off any items that run more than $400 or $500. Many big stars do. Your good friend Beyonce is going to buy you that stuff regardless.

Shopping for People for Your Baby

As an A-list star, you need not shop for baby things. You already have way too many people killing themselves to buy you $250 Moses baskets and organic blankets from Bel Bambini—the other Petit Tresor, in case you don't know that already. However, you *do* need to purchase some people. Here, courtesy of several celebrity staffing firms and nannies, comes your own checklist of people you must collect before you head off for your C-section.

Professional Baby-Proofer: Didn't know they had those? Ouch. Time to fire your publicist. The professional baby-proofer provides services that, in other parts of the country, un-famous parents must perform themselves. That includes installing magnetic cabinet locks in the White Marble Room and applying doorknob plugs in the Pink Marble Room. The proofer is not to be confused with the nursery decorator *or* the helpmeet who handles the personal fitting for the nursing bra.

Nursery Decorator: You may feel some pressure to provide a lavish room for your new baby. Indulge this fear sooner rather than later. Otherwise the people providing your free or deeply discounted nursery decor will have to rush your order, likely misspelling your child's name on the wall murals and chandeliers. Hire a decorator who understands your value and who will insist on building the most lavish nursery that *People* magazine has ever paid to see.[39]

At-Home Birthing Coach: It's a known fact that hospitals have germs, which can make ordinary people sick, and which may or may not have deadly effects on the particularly artistic and sensitive children of the famous. In leaving your home to attend birthing classes or prenatal yoga instruction, you also run the risk of some sort of fan stampede. Avoid those hazards and go the A-list route by hiring a personal, private birthing coach. The coach visits your ranch, compound, or gated manse at your convenience. She will likely spend several minutes early in the meeting amusing you with instructions on how to "push"—the usual infant-dispelling method employed by the rustic peoples of other states and nations. You of course will have a conveniently scheduled cesarean

---

[39] **Learn more** on your cream and gold luxury nursery on page 95.

section, but you always appreciate any effort to connect with your fans. The personal coach may also show you birthing films and other visuals that you would normally see on a standard-definition monitor at a hospital-run prenatal class.

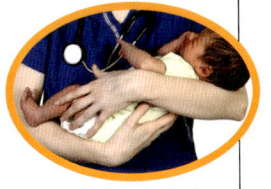

This hospital nurse had better not be making direct eye contact with your baby.

A Charming Dweeb to Install All the Cameras.
You love cameras, and the camera loves you. Dozens of tiny spy cameras will love your nanny, too. Or, if hidden well enough, they'll nail her dead to rights if she touches even one of your forty pairs of Paige Premium Denim jeans. (Or if she upsets your child.) Install spy cameras in every room in the house and then casually inform the nanny. Let her wonder whether there are any hidden cameras in the bathroom. You wouldn't be the first celebrity to wire the toilet. According to nannies who would rather not be ~~sued~~ named, even sports stars—who, for the record, are not A-list celebrities—have done this.

The Neonatal Nurse:
For a mere $400 to $500 per day, you can hire a round-the-clock person, or a two- to three-person team, to step in as soon as your baby is delivered. No need to get up every two hours to feed your little gene bearer; just pump your milk and let the neonatal nurse slog it out. The nurse will also put your baby on a feeding and sleeping schedule, and stay with you in your ranch, compound, or gated manse for roughly six to ten weeks. Not to be confused with the ...

Fashion Stylist:
They're not just for red carpets and "private" lunches at Mr. Chow! Now that you're officially fat postnatal, you'll need some roomy size-four clothes, and any good wardrobe advisor should have some fashionable transition pieces handy. Plan on wearing your post-pregnantitis wardrobe for perhaps two months at most. After that, *People* magazine is going to start howling for its "body after baby" interview, and you'll need to fit into leather Versace pants for the cover.

Various and Sundry Extra People. Just to Have.
When was the last time you were completely alone? Exactly. And it's extremely risky to change that habit now that you've just given birth. So recruit a few more folks to ensure that you never have to spend a minute alone with your baby. According to nannies in the know—and under current nondisclosure agreements—other stars sure have.

Custom Shoes
and Other Necessities:
Decorating Your Baby

Your work is far from over. You must now turn your attention to your baby's nursery and the high expectations therein. Just kidding. You don't need to do anything. If you've done your job and befriended a couple of couturiers—you have, haven't you? Again: Publicist—then the baby clothing will come to you. As long as you agree to Instagram the hell out of all of the gifts you get, you'll get gifts. Trust. How do I know this? Because even Kim Kardashian's baby gets this stuff. Giuseppe Zanotti crafted two pairs of custom baby shoes for little North West, who is also a grandee of Charlotte Olympia, Hermès, and other labels.

How do I know this? Instagram. Pay attention.

Emergency Scenario:

You Need an $8,300 Crib Handmade by Florentine Craftsmen

Once your baby is born, there are bound to be instances when your nanny, who, after all, is only human, succumbs to arm cradle fatigue. Of course, you yourself can't be expected to drop everything else to hold said infant, because you are saving your strength for maternal displays when paparazzi are present. You need an appropriate place to drop that child. You need a $8,300 crib handmade by craftsmen in Italy.

As luck would have it, such a crib exists. We know this because your fellow celebrities also love to register for cribs made by the same folk: a company called Notte Fatata. At Notte Fatata, workers wear suits even when they do manual labor, including the inlay of gold leaf onto their products. That is not an exaggeration.

Fellow movie stars such as Emily Blunt, as well as your fashionista bestie Victoria Beckham, know where to get such essentials for babies: a shop—actually a shoppe—called Petit Tresor near Los Angeles. Your future best friend Kate Middleton also reportedly eyed Notte Fatata before giving birth to Prince George. A crib that once fell under the eyes of royalty: Yep, you definitely need that piece of furniture. Get it before Kim Kardashian does.

In fact, get several. According to the folks at Petit Tresor, pregnant celebrities often register for multiples of everything. Multiple houses, you understand. And multiple decors. As a spokeswoman for Petit Tresor once told me, singer-turned-fashion-designer Gwen Stefani "lived in a baroque looking house" when she had one of her sons, so for that jaunt, "she wanted everything black and white to match that style—the baby's clothes, the furniture, all the toys, everything."

Emergency Scenario:

Your Child Has Peed on Its $235 Cashmere Blanket

Take small comfort in the following fact: You are not alone. Hollywood nannies say that many children of celebrities develop a bedwetting habit. The nannies suspect it comes from a lack of parental attention, which is, of course, ridiculous, given that you, like most celebrities, offer a generous one hour per day of your time, on average, to your children. Consider taking a vacation with your child to show you care. Nannies estimate that celebrities spend up to—not a misprint, not a myth— four hours daily with their children when on vacation. That should solve everything.

Wait Until the Last Minute to Finalize Your Nursery Theme

Always take your time in designing your child's nursery. True, the stocky peoples of the American hinterlands must typically wait at least twelve weeks for their custom baby furniture to arrive. Those parents-to-be carry no interest to *People* magazine—unless they are about to produce septuplets who survived a mine collapse while rescuing a litter of Scottish-fold kittens.

Your pull with the media means that businesses will bend time and space to please you, even at the last minute. Why? Because they want their wares to appear in magazine spreads detailing your glorious nursery. Go ahead and dither over your nursery decor until, say, a week or two before your big magazine photo shoot. Your inner eye cannot be rushed, anyway. The suppliers will likely stay up all night customizing your baby's nursery furniture, singing traditional arias as they cheerfully tap their little wooden mallets and nod to and fro in their pointed felt caps.

If some aspect of the nursery still displeases you, do what one celebrity wife did recently and simply cancel the magazine photo shoot. Call the furniture makers the next day, rouse them from their childlike slumber, and inform them that the custom bedding never arrived, and the shoot has been canceled. They will always take the news with good cheer, joyously smashing their tiny mallets on whatever they find handy.

The Secret Nanny-to-Child Ratio You Must Know

According to celebrity nannies, stars employ an average of three (3) nannies per one (1) child: a day nanny, a night nanny, and a weekend or travel nanny. A lucky nanny earns roughly $30 to $40 an hour.

If this expense seems excessive, given that you haven't paid for a pair of sneakers since your pilot-season days staying at the Oakwood apartments,[40] know this: Even a common daytime drama player has an average of two nannies per child, one for the week and another for the weekend. And you, of course, are no common daytime drama player.

This unfortunate and unknown woman has no nanny to take her child to its chiropractor.

A qualified nanny can offer full-service childcare such that you *never have to touch or speak to your infant.* If your nanny at any time asks you to interface with your child, dismiss her immediately and adopt another (nanny). The fired nanny will not blame you; most have been bred to expect a firing every three weeks. According to nannies contacted for this secret survival guide, their responsibilities typically include:

[40] A cluster of temporary living spaces occupied by Hollywood wannabes before they find success. **Tom Cruise** and **Hilary Duff** used to live there.

- Bathing the child
- Packing lunch, or …
- Coordinating with the house chef to determine what the child will eat
- Picking up after the child
- Completing homework assignments
- Dressing the child
- Brushing the child's teeth
- Packing the child's luggage for trips with the travel nanny
- Preparing all home meals
- Playing games and reading bedtime stories
- Transporting the child to classes or school
- Transporting the child to its chiropractor, acupuncturist, or therapist
- Handling aspects of any party or activity the child is hosting, such as birthdays
- Purchasing gifts on behalf of the child
- Shopping for the child's wardrobe
- Comforting the child when it suffers from nightmares or night terrors
- Putting the child down for naps

To make your situation completely clear: Employing any fewer than three (3) nannies per child significantly increases your risk of having to carry, bathe, feed, speak to, soothe, read to, dress, toilet train, praise, or in some other way interact with your child. These tasks are not your job—unless

a reporter for *Vogue* is visiting. Then it is *always* your job, and there is *nothing* you love more. Not even the immortal art of film.

[41] **Then again,** the number of nannies you employ is in indirect proportion to your chances of contracting foot-and-mouth disease or having to change a diaper. Sometimes math is mean.

Emergency Scenario:

You Have No Recipe for Tacos

On rare occasions, a cover writer for *Vogue* or some other serious news outlet will want to observe you cooking dinner for your children. If your publicist forgets to warn you about this in advance, here is a recipe for tacos. Kate Hudson once valiantly faced down her own mealtime challenge under the merciless gaze of a *Vogue* reporter and even managed to say a few words to her son, Ryder, during the ordeal. Though she ultimately prepared steak and fries, the conversation focused on another favorite mother-and-son dish: tacos.

"What's my specialty?" Kate asks him.
"What does Mommy make all the time"
Ryder hesitates.
"What does Mommy make a lot of?"
He's got it: "Money!" he says . . . .
"Mommy's tacos!" she corrects.

—Vogue, January 200

Kate Hudson, gourmand.

Your children probably love tacos. Confirm that fact with your nannies before proceeding.

~~Night Nanny's~~ Mummy's Tacos

1 pound lean ground meat (beef, turkey, buffalo, or chicken)
3 to 5 tbsp Mexican spices (procured by assistant during last-minute shopping run)
2 cups lettuce, shredded
1 cup sharp cheddar cheese or Tofu-rella, shredded
3 tomatoes, diced
1 package crunchy taco shells

Allow assistant to brown and season meat as you shred the cheese and the lettuce in the Cuisinart in view of the reporter.[42] Allow the reporter to dice the tomatoes, as it will allow her to feel like she's a part of your incredible family for a short, golden time. Have the children sit at the kitchen table and sing about how much they love Night Nanny's tacos. Explain to the reporter that Night Nanny is "Mummy's nickname." Serve immediately.

---

[42] **Insert cheese** in feed tube. Push button. Remove cheese. Insert lettuce in feed tube. Push button. Remove lettuce.

CHAPTER SIX

Venturing Outside the Compound

Surviving Any Foray, From a Short Errand to Overnight Travel—or Avoiding It Altogether

As I write this, my head thrums with awe over the bravery I have witnessed as a member of the elite Hollywood press corps. I have seen Christian Bale forsake the security of his private home and venture forth into the wilds of the Four Seasons Hotel in Beverly Hills. He hacked through suite after suite as the press rocketed questions about exactly how amazing it was to work with director Christopher Nolan. He never once faltered.

I have observed Salma Hayek go forth strongly from the door of the Fred Segal boutique and venture toward her car parked several yards away, completely unarmed. I have witnessed Madonna brave a dinner with only a half-dozen friends to ensure her comfort and safety. I have gazed, tears in my jaded eyes, as Nicole Kidman traveled from one floor of the Beverly Hills Hotel to another floor of the Beverly Hills Hotel—and survived. I've seen Lea Michele stand in line for snacks at a movie theater, by all that is holy and may the saints preserve her.

My point is this: If these luminaries of the twenty-first century can walk out of their homes and mingle for minutes among ordinary people who could approach them at any time and for any reason, so can you. Just think of what your life coach told you the other day: You can do anything, even if it involves a trip to the DMV. In this chapter, you will learn how to perform any task that involves traveling beyond your comfort zone.

The Perils of Car Travel

A properly outfitted car may seem like an ideal means of escape from a besieged, or simply boring, compound. The height of an SUV limits visibility just enough to provide plausible deniability in case a paparazzo accuses you of knowingly running over his feet. And a custom grille on a Maybach or Phantom can leave wonderfully fanciful patterns on any paparazzi you do

Emergency Scenario:

You Run Low on Gas

Give your business manager a break and tell him there's no need to send over another car from the dealership. Pull over to the nearest gas station and enlist a paparazzo to pump the gas. The method has worked well for Britney Spears, though there is no need to think of such people during this ordeal.

"accidentally" hit—a fine conversation piece for your next Oscar after-party.

Still, abandon this fantasy at once. Never, ever count on driving your car to freedom from anything. The weakness in this plan comes not from any fault in your car's engineering, but through the people lurking closest to you, namely, your own bodyguards.

High-quality security personnel[44] often require their clients to forgo driving—and at the least convenient times. The best security experts are often small and quite narrow-shouldered, but do not engage them physically if they attempt to banish you to the backseat. Your more disciplined bodyguards have mastered the art of instant recall, remembering, for example, that you ate only three pieces of macaroni last night at Kitchen 24 and are running only on the residual fumes. They will not hesitate to wear you down until you feel faint, snatch away your keys in the flash of one raccoon-like paw, and spend the next half hour chittering away at you about "last week's DUI," all the while oblivious to your searing white hot tears and blinding psychic pain.

Mental tactics also tend to fall flat on higher-end security types. Your stylist and three assistants have assured you, time and again, of your amazing skills at everything—cooking, children's book writing, and, of course, driving. They all know not to interfere with your right to drive, which, according to your attorney, is clearly marked in the Constitution. Elite protectors care nothing for the law. They also care nothing for your image—the fact that most of your A-list friends simply

★★★★A-List Tip

How to Purchase a Car

Sometimes the entire world seems bent on crushing you and your fellow unassuming bohemians in the A-list community. Most of the time you have some way of fighting back, but not always. Sometimes you'll just have to pay to buy your own car. Unless you have an endorsement deal with a carmaker, such as Tiger Woods's deal with Buick[46], your dealer will probably take advantage of local commerce law and make you pay—occasionally even full price—for your next set of wheels. (Even legends like Dustin Hoffman have been known to pay retail value for a car with no negotiation.) Most of the time, they want the entire balance up front, via check or cash. Please don't get too excited if the dealer offers to wash and detail your car before you take it off the lot. Dealers do that for everyone.

[44] **See more on** the proper type of security personnel for A-listers on page 116.

must drive their own cars if they want people to understand just how much they paid for them. If you submit to a driver, people might think the car belongs to the chauffeur company. That's $450,000 in bragging rights down the drain. Then again, security experts also remain unimpressed by math.

If you insist on doing your own driving—and, really, what A-lister doesn't?—you may have to fire your elite security person and temporarily hire a more malleable type of body-guard[45] Otherwise, resign yourself to spending an additional $65,000 to $125,000 a year for a little man who gets to have all the fun with the pedals and the stereo.

Escape Via Long-Haul Air Travel:
Flying While Famous

This one's important. Put down your cell phone and your other cell phone for a minute and give me your full attention. At the risk of scaring you, what I am about to tell you could be the most vital piece of information you garner from this entire survival guide. Nothing may be more important than what you are about to read.

The airplane people are out to completely destroy you, one disastrous New York-to-Miami flight at a time.

No one seems to discriminate more against your class than airlines and their stygian cohorts, the airports. Do not be charmed by the way they butterfly your shrimp in first class, flaying and folding each little sea creature to look like an

[45] **See more on** Club Cubes on page 34.

entirely different little sea creature. The sushi chefs living inside the jet probably do the same thing for their own lucky and pampered children once they clock out of work.

Just because airlines pull bunches of strings so that you don't have to board any plane until the very last minute, and just because they always clear a special, gawper-free area for you in the VIP airport lounge, does not mean that airport workers harbor any sort of admiration for you. Just the opposite. Everybody—from the man who dances with those handheld paddles out on the tarmac, all the way up to that living cadaver who runs American Airlines—is plotting against you. They might be huddling right now in a subterranean tunnel beneath LAX, sucking the marrow out of kitten bones and brainstorming ways to break you. That is, if they aren't dropping everything to help you jump ahead of the line and make that tight connection to Cannes. Even then, while they're mowing down every living beast standing between you and your next flight, they're probably thinking about ways to crush your spirit in their slavering jaws—your spirit and that of your dear friends Jennifer Lawrence and Brad Pitt.

Analysts aren't exactly sure what the airline industry has against you and the thirty good friends who travel with you—the ones sitting back in business class and requesting seventy-five free Bloody Marys—but the proof of long-standing hostility is irrefutable.

For the first time, the complete evidence has been compiled, and the solutions revealed.

Los Angeles International Airport. Be afraid. Be very afraid.

EXHIBIT A: Gwen Stefani
Assaulted in Baggage Claim

The Details:

IT MAY HAVE OCCURRED somewhere between her first wedding ceremony in London and her second set of vows in Los Angeles, or it may have been *after* the second ceremony, and sometime around the honeymoon. The details are hazy, but at one point, right around that general time, Gwen Stefani and That Man She Married were accosted in an airport baggage claim by a celebrity-magazine reporter and asked to give an interview. The reporter has a reputation for being professional, polite, and even friendly, and Stefani gladly gave the interview, but that is all beside the point. Gwen Stefani, who *isn't even a B-lister*, was *boldly walked up to* in an *airport* by a person whose *only authority* to approach her rested in an *ugly, brown document* forged by *dead men* during the Constitutional Convention. *Tenuous justification, at best.* Was a rogue band of baggage handlers behind this daring frontal attack? Will anyone ever really know?[47]

Gwen Stefani: singer, wife, mother, survivor.

Solution:

SEE THE DETAILED tactics under Exhibit A for the most efficient recommended approach. Or, two possible alternatives, both of which are used all the time by A-listers:

- Have your assistant wait in baggage claim in your stead.

- Consider a professional baggage transport company like Luggage Free. The more egalitarian companies offer door-to-door services for anybody: A-listers, CEOs—even

[47] Doesn't **Gwen** have enough problems, what with her husband having been born with no lips like Melissa Etheridge? Can't God pick on someone else for one rotten minute?

anonymous strugglers like Pierce Brosnan, who has used Luggage Free and has endorsed it. Such companies arrive at your home, brownstone, compound, or faux ranch, pick up your luggage, wrap it for extra protection, and ship it ahead of your trip. The luggage then arrives at your hotel or private island relatively unscathed, not counting whatever oils or microscopic skin flakes might be left behind by the transport workers. Needless to say, you get to avoid baggage claim and whatever bold siege the handlers may be plotting at this very second.

EXHIBIT B:
Mariah Carey's Dog

The Details:

SEVERAL YEARS AGO, Mariah Carey had a Jack Russell terrier. The dog's name was Jackson P. Mutley; the two of them had a special bond that no other man or beast or life coach could possibly understand. Mariah may still have Jack, or perhaps he began to stifle her growth as an artist, and she had to make a break– a common development. But let's not get

Not Jackson P. Mutley. This is an animal actor cast for re-enactment purposes only.

sidetracked. Mariah had a dog named Jack. When the singer had to fly from New York to Los Angeles, she tried to book an additional first-class seat for Jack. However, the airline refused. According to Carey, who later relayed the disaster to British *Glamour*, the airline told her that the dog was "too big" for his own seat and "wasn't famous enough"[48] to merit an exception. The airline workers responsible for this incident are still at large; the airline still flies its planes with impunity every single day.

---

[48] **In fairness,** the airline may have a point when it comes to the fame argument. Even though he has his own blog on MySpace, Mr. Mutley is not famous, at least, not outside Japan, where at least one fan blog has been launched in his honor. Even Mr. Mutley's owner, whose voice can make the stone beard of the Lincoln Memorial bleed, is not an A-lister. See page 114 for details on A-list pet travel.

Solution:

SHOULD THIS KIND OF DISASTER happen to you, and you are within a day's drive of your pet, you may try having the animal messengered to you via a pet transport service. (See more on pet transport services on page 114.) As a last resort, you may use Mariah's approach and have your driver transport the dog cross-country to you in your Mercedes. Because, yes, stars really do that.

EXHIBIT C: Brad Pitt
Forced to Undergo Airport Security

YES: THE EXACT SAME AIRPORT security area that processes the Dorito-eating general populace. The violation of Mr. Pitt's rights occurred when the actor reportedly arrived at Chicago's O'Hare airport to catch a commercial flight. A crowd gathered as Pitt prepared to go through a security checkpoint, so a rep from the Transportation Security Administration emerged to escort poor Mr. Pitt through a private screening area. By then, Mr. Pitt was most likely permanently scarred.

If you fly on a major or even minor airline, you, too, will have to go through that same security rigamarole—even if you're Jack Nicholson, and you're so decrepit and laden with Oscars you can barely crawl through a metal detector. Granted, your A-list status may buy you a private queue, or even a separate room, for your security processing, just like Pitt got. But still. Not enough. Not nearly enough.

Brad Pitt braved a commercial air flight—and survived.

Solution:

TWO WORDS: Private jet. Sure, it can cost, say, $25,000 for a single trip from Los Angeles to New York—or even $50,000 or $100,000 if you really like to travel in style. Then again, people who fly on private jets do not have to submit to airport security. Charter companies usually provide the names of their clients to the Transportation Security Administration for prescreening. That means that you, the A-lister, can simply pull up on the tarmac, allow an assistant or some other little person to toss your Louis Vuitton luggage into the hold, step on board, and take off. No strangers rummaging through the winding recesses of your Birkin bag. No metal detectors. Just you and your custom-catered menu from Wolfgang Puck or Nobu.

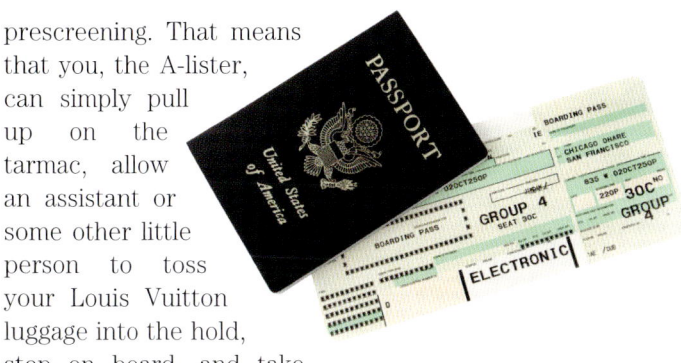

A charter company with enough celebrity experience also knows how to thwart paparazzi who like to lurk in airports. Jet pilots may delay submitting your name to the TSA until the very last possible minute. They may also change your registered flight plan in midair to keep the press guessing—whatever it takes to keep your privacy from being bruised.

Emergency Scenario:

Your Assistant Forgot to Bring Your Dog on the Plane

First things first: Call your agent and tell her that every contract you sign from now on will require whoever hires you—the studio, the production company, the cosmetics giant—to pay to ship your dog to the set, or wherever you are required to travel for work. Many, many stars, including Orlando Bloom, do this, using a dedicated animal hauling service such as Pacific Pet Transport. (PPT also ships movie animals, such as rattlesnakes, poison dart frogs, and potato bugs to filming locations, but there is no need to think of such ugly things during this traumatic and dark episode in your life.) Some actors have been known to pay for their own dog shipment; Kate Bosworth, it is said, dug into the pockets of her own slim-fit capris to have her dog sent to Australia while she shot scenes for *Superman Returns.* The dog was put in a monthlong quarantine first, I am told, but the filming took much longer, so it all worked out A-OK!

Still. You're no middling bobbleheaded starlet like Bosworth. You really ought to have Warner Bros. or Sony pay for your pet shipments. The shipping service will pick up your dog at any of your usual haunts, such as your manager's office or the Chateau Marmont, and take care of all documentation, blood work, and the like. The dog is then boarded onto a commercial airline flight. Finally, another agent hand-delivers your dog to the final destination. The service isn't cheap—a simple, door-to-door, New York-to-Los Angeles transport for a Golden Retriever starts at a few grand—but really. There is no telling what might happen to your acting ability if your Yorkie isn't around to sit on your exquisitely etched belly while you get your facials. It really is a small price for the head of Sony to pay, and, even if she screams at your agent for four hours indicating otherwise, deep down, she knows it.

Firing your assistant is optional. In any case, fire your publicist.

Recruiting Security
from the Native Population

Something tells me that Kate Upton has no problem recruiting bodyguards whenever she goes to the beach.

As an A-list celebrity, you probably fear venturing out of your home alone. Most of your high-powered friends have grown so used to having people around them that they suffer mild hallucinations when they are by themselves. They may even hire people just to keep them company and to fetch the occasional thingy from the what's-it-called while they're busy chewing a nail.

Even when you have no entourage or security personnel on hand, you're never without allies. In fact, traveling solo, even on foot, can prove safe and even entertaining if you know how to recruit a last-minute bodyguard, or ten, from the surrounding environs.

The best places to harvest some native security include surf spots, neighborhood pickup basketball games, and any other place likely to carry a large population of well-toned men under forty. Should you fall under sudden attack from paparazzi, resist the natural urge to display annoyance or disapproval. Your friend Gwyneth has tried that with the paps a few times, and she just ends up looking more iguana-like than usual. Instead stand very still, taking care not to show your teeth, which can indicate hostility.

The nearby males will cease their leisure activities and rush to your assistance as fervently as if you had just suffered a hail of hollow-point bullets fired by dozens of poisonous lionfish. Millions of would-be gladiators in the greater Los Angeles basin labor under the delusion that they somehow know you. Remember that time you accidentally made eye contact with that scrub in the ironic trucker hat on the beach at Malibu? No? *He* does. As far as concerns the quaintly but usefully misguided lads who breathe the same particulate Los Angeles oxygen as you, they are *all* Spartacus[49]. … or McConaughey. As such, they must chivalrously protect you—one of their "own"—from all physical and moral threats. That includes the greatest non-nuclear threat of all: paparazzi. (Including the paps you called yesterday to tip off about where you'd be frolicking with your toddler that afternoon.) These young men understand the dire danger that paparazzi pose to your image, which is pretty much as important as your heart or lungs. Much like the members of your entourage, they also crave the elevation of self-esteem that comes only through serving a member of Legend Community. By all means, don't let the natives down. Don't make direct eye contact, but don't flee, either.

First the local men will threaten the paparazzi, barking quaint phrases about how you are "just like everyone else" and should be treated "just like everyone else." Maybe these guys didn't see they way you glowed like an archangel in that last J.J. Abrams movie, but do not interrupt their war chants to correct them. The paparazzi may counter with something about the First Amendment, which is ironic, because most paps will be spouting these silly "freedom of assembly" platitudes with a cockney British accent. Eventually the young athletes will bloody the lethal cameramen and drive them off.[50]

Once the show has ended, move on before you must speak to your rescuers.

[49] **This is an obscure** reference to an old-timey movie starring a venerable A-list ancestor of yours.

[50] In the summer of 2008, two paparazzi attempted to photograph Matthew McConaughey while he surfed on a public beach in Malibu. About thirteen valiant surfer dudes formed a semicircle around the paps and ordered them to take their leave, posthaste (or words to that effect). According to subsequent reports, one photographer suffered a broken nose, and another was tossed into the ocean.

Defending Your Schedule: Using Your Fame To Escape Any Obligation

When it comes to escaping undesirable tasks, no escape tool has proven more effective than your own recognizance. Although stashing a .357 Magnum in your handbag may seem the most logical choice in any crisis situation, including the *absolute rape* of your jam-packed schedule by unsympathetic underlings, guns can prove more hazard than help. One wrong move, and the gun could end up in the hands of your paparazzi attacker, who may then return fire by photographing the Magnum and selling the image to a magazine.

Unlike a gun, which requires a bodyguard to fire, fame needs no ammunition, cleaning, training, or special storage. It also requires no license; the government needs to know when you have a gun, but it has no way to ascertain that you possess fame, unless the government reads *US Weekly.* And it doesn't.

As an A-lister, there's no reason you should have to stand in line to see the pope. He should be standing in line to see you.

It reads those tedious political journals, and possibly *Redbook.* At the time this book was going to print, licenses for fame were not required by any federal, state, or local government.

Your stardom is one well-honed weapon. Always know the strengths of your fame and how to deploy it. Also know its limitations. Fame can provide efficient escapes from jury duty, airport security delays, and the lines at your local Department of Motor Vehicles, but it tends to lose its hassle-evaporating qualities when faced with a mortgage.

Avoiding Jury Duty

Every so often you may receive a statement in the mail saying you have been selected to serve on a jury. The law requires you to heed this call and report to your local courthouse. There you will ostensibly serve the "justice system," and perhaps even the "criminal justice system," though survivors of this experience have reported disappointingly few similarities with the Emmy award–winning *Law & Order*.

A-listers who enter this "jury duty" scenario unprepared may be ushered into a large pen, or roomlike enclosure, where they are stored along with average people to await further instruction. In extreme circumstances, celebrities may be herded, in dangerous proximity to the unfamous citizenry, into a courtroom. There, lawyers and judges may submit them to questions, supposedly about potential "bias," *all without a publicist present.*

The easiest way to dodge this snake pit is to avoid registering to vote. You have a right to vote, of course, but you can do much, much more for your country by endorsing a presidential candidate or holding a fund-raiser with your good friend George Clooney. However, if you were so foolish as to exercise your voting rights in the past, it may be too late. The jury duty database probably has you in its clacking pincers by now. Applying for a driver's license can also make you vulnerable to jury summons, depending on the state you live in.

Cameron Diaz: Five-second juror. Dismissed!

If you employ a sizable staff, make sure than one of them runs regular interference between you and your mail. According to judges and defense lawyers contacted by this writer, most jurisdictions do a fairly lax job at enforcing jury summonses. After all, the logic goes, a summons usually arrives via U.S. Mail. All you have to do is say it never came—blaming the aforementioned staffer you have assigned to mail interception duty—and, usually, there is little anyone can do. Your lackey simply tosses the summons in the trash to let it rot among the empty Xanax bottles and splits of Cristal, assuring the boss that nothing more will come of it.

Yes, your underling's actions may trigger the threat of contempt of court. The court may try to reach you again, this time through certified mail. If your assistant should "lose" that piece with the rest of the junk

Nice try with the bohemian drifter disguise, Ashton. We all know it's you. Now get down to the courthouse so you can Tweet that you're there.

mail, you can always issue a public apology and fire your assistant (and your publicist, while you're at it).

Still, if facing contempt of court—or the contempt of anyone—frightens you, you have not exhausted your options.

In field studies, fame has proven itself as an effective weapon against jury duty. Gloria Estefan once arrived in court, bodyguard in tow, to perform her civic duty. She signed more than a dozen autographs as she waited, trapped among the mouth breathers surrounding her. But she was quickly dismissed over fears that she would spur a media circus.

Judges tend to see famous figures as unwelcome distractions. Fans, paparazzi, and other press may disrupt proceedings. Other potential jurors also may find concentration impossible in the presence of your flawless, makeup-free complexion and adorable Charlotte Olympia flats and that *je ne sais quois* that Woody Allen finds so *incredible*.

The day before you must report for duty, have your assistant or publicist inform the paparazzi and provide directions to the courthouse if necessary. (The paps may have trouble getting through the metal detectors, but that's their problem.) Short of injury, make sure you suffer as much difficulty as possible reaching the front door. Bring an entourage of at least eight. The posse may face ejection by the judge, but by that time, the point should be quite clear: Living legends in the jury box are more trouble than they're worth.

Other successful applications of fame vs. jury duty include Carmen Electra, who apparently served one day before her celebrity status kicked in; Diddy, who, according to media reports, arrived with an entourage; and Cameron Diaz, resplendent in workout gear. Charlie Sheen also recently reported for jury duty but was dismissed without being empaneled. It's a known fact that defense attorneys have a bias against warlocks with tiger blood.

In some very rare circumstances, you may want to consider braving the jury duty experience, especially when a fellow celebrity faces a threat to his or her well-being. During jury selection for the Robert Blake trial, comedian Harry Shearer and actress Christina Applegate both, coincidentally, received jury summonses and reported for duty. Neither entertainer was chosen, and Blake later won an acquittal, but the presence of two fellow sort-of celebrities most certainly would have served as a balm to the simian-faced suspect, or at least calmed him enough to smooth out some of those unfortunate facial fjords.

Should you need a guide to courtroom etiquette, may we suggest Lindsey Lohan.

Your Fame vs. the Line at the DMV: A Fight You Can Win

Most of your fellow members of the Legend Community harbor a distinct fear of their local Department of Motor Vehicles office. The long lines, the waiting the possibility of being photographed without any decent lighting—the experience can range from merely foreign to utterly terrifying. Adding to the anxiety is the fact that even famous people must report to the DMV in person if they need

Keep your cool in the fiery circles of Hell—excuse me: the DMV—by channeling the uncompromising power of Samuel L. Jackson.

a new driver's license; no assistant or friend can appear in your stead. Not even your supremely talented and beloved colleague Samuel L. Jackson.

Unfamous people have developed a certain numbness to the DMV experience, spurred by the fact that, for most of them, no amount of soft lighting could help anyway. However, you have other options.

Do not be afraid to wield your fame in your defense. As with jury duty, DMV offices generally dislike disruptions and will go to great lengths to avoid them. For example, many celebrities have leveraged their fame into commandeering a back door or secret entrance to their local DMV, mainly so that administrators can avoid any sort of mob scene. A publicist or assistant usually calls the office in advance to secure the VIP entrance.

Britney Spears was able to wait for her license in her car after briefly braving the DMV's dank interior. A DMV worker walked the license out to her vehicle and handed it to her through the car window. (Let's remember that Britney Spears isn't even a movie star[51] like you.) During his post–*American Idol*-flat-iron-obsession period, Clay Aiken once got to cut to the front of a DMV line.[52] And when he got his first drivers license, Justin Bieber reportedly got to cut in line at the Atlanta DMV. (Bonus fact: He also, apparently, got his choice of several photos. For the record, infamous people usually have to settle for whatever the DMV hands them.)

[51] **You may wonder** if *Crossroads* counts as a film. It does not.

[52] See the previous entry on avoiding jury duty for specific fame-related strategies, including use of paparazzi and entourages.

CHAPTER SEVEN

Your Money

Earning It, Keeping It, and Using Your Fame to Pay for as Little as Possible

Money is scary, isn't it, the way it always has to involve numbers? Creatives never do well with numbers. The mere idea of adding and subtracting can stress you so hard that your neck puckers and you have to summon your facialist back to your house to drain your lymph nodes all over again. For an A-lister, the anxiety and uncertainty you suffer in the name of your money comes on a grand scale. The rest of America has no idea of the monumental challenges you face as a major earner.

For one, there's the mysterious and terrifying "$1 million" bill. You've never seen one, but surely it must exist. And wherever these million-dollar bills are, they must carry an awesome and spectacular power, capable of bringing about a new age of people, or unspeakable evil. How else does Giorgio Armani bribe the maître d' at Versailles? (Briefcases of bills are so Clooney caper movie. Try greasing the palm of a maître d' with a Louis Vuitton attache. It doesn't fit.). And who is on the $1 million bill? Possibly President Andrew Shepherd, whose timeless romance with Annette Bening saved the environment at the end of that historical biography starring Michael Douglas. History is so fascinating.

Back to the money. Adding to the intimidation you feel about your money: the fuzziness of it all. Your financial worth is more complicated than the economies of many small nations, yet you have no idea where all of it goes. Your business managers tell you they have your personal GNP well under control, but that's probably what the great Charlton Heston was told before an employee at his business management firm plead no contest to embezzling $700,000 of his money.

So where does it all go? Why won't they let you touch all of it at once, just to reassure yourself that it is real? For you, money maintenance may seem like an abstract entity, sort of like "washing" a car or "reading" to a child.

Resist the urge to collapse into a twitching thicket of nerves when thinking about your money. Have your assistant remind you as often as necessary: You have retained people—business managers, accountants, lawyers—whose sole purpose lies in taming your money. Making it multiply and morph into beautiful items, such as cars and limited-edition BlackBerry phones dolled up in diamonds.

The average A-list celebrity only ends up with perhaps $3 million of a hypothetical $10 million paycheck. A good chunk of the $7 million goes to your people, of course, including your agent, who is a dear friend, and your publicist, who is your best friend, and your assistant, who is firing your publicist next week. No wonder you have so many questions about where your money goes. The following should serve as a dense but brief practical guide to your money.

Master it, and you'll never fear the unseen $1 million bill again. According to media reports, your adorable indie-actress friend Christina Ricci was told by her business managers to stop buying clothes, furs, and jewelry because she was spending too much. If she had read what I'm about to present to you, she would have known that she could have gotten many of those basic household items for free or at a deep discount, using nothing but the baby-doll charm emanating from her anime eyes and a single call from her throat-chewing New York publicist.

Like her famous Aunt Julia before her, Emma Roberts is learning that the higher your star ascends, the taller your pile of luxury swag will be.

Know a Minion:
Who Takes What

Every A-lister retains an array of financial and career management underlings. Many of them operate out of airy faux-Asian offices strewn with primitive art objects and extremely important black-and-white portraiture. Other power minions prefer a more nomadic existence requiring little more than a Bluetooth headset and leased Audi A6. Of course, the money for those Audis and primitive art objects always comes from your own pockets, via percentages taken out of your $10 million to $20 million-per-film acting salary. (Unless you agree to a back-end deal. For those arrangements, you forego a salary and instead agree to take your pay out of the film's gross or profit. In that case, you could end up making $42 million for a single film, like your friend Cameron Diaz did for Bad Teacher.) But such is the cruelty of modern man. Professionals cost money.

It's normal to harbor the occasional worry that your team may be bilking you. How many Zen gardens and smoked-glass fountains can these people afford on their own, anyway?[53] Below

---

[53] **That's not a** rhetorical question. Agents take roughly 10 percent of your $15 million-per-film fee. That's $1.5 million. A Zen garden starts at about $250 for a large rake and some sand. Your agent can therefore afford roughly six thousand Zen gardens every time you film a blockbuster.

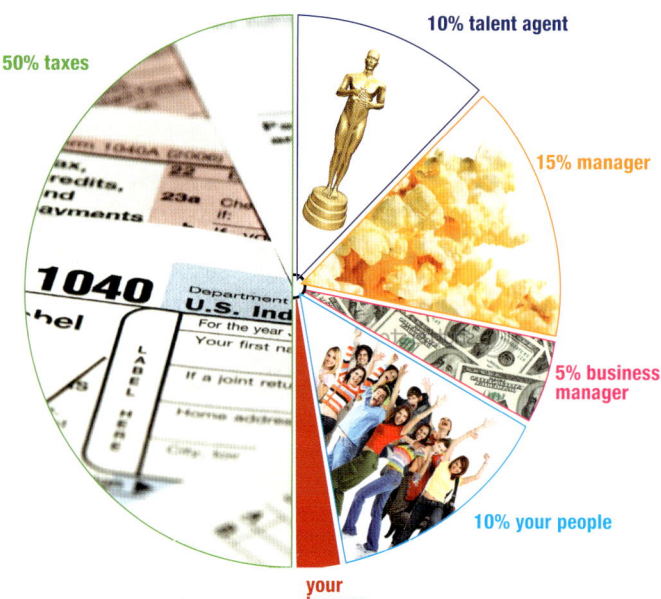

50% taxes

10% talent agent

15% manager

5% business manager

10% your people

your income

Don't panic! This graph is **not** drawn to scale. You earn more than this, but your business manager doesn't want you to know that.

you'll find a handy guide to your chipper underlings, including the function of each and how much they typically take out of your paychecks.[54]

1. Your talent agent: 10 percent. The talent agent fields your deal offers, seeks out others, and makes sure you receive maximum pay for the projects you take. More powerful agencies can tap into their impressive rosters of directors, writers, producers, and cinematographers to "package" projects around you. They can score you a killer role in an Oscar prestige film by pairing you with some legendary director, whom, of course, they also happen to represent. Do not confuse the talent agent with the commercial agent or the voice-over agent. Unless it makes you happy, sweetheart. In that case, seriously, babe, call them all whatever you want.

---

[54] We use that term loosely. As a movie star, you receive pay every week for the duration of a movie shoot. If you make $15 million for a film, and the film takes eight weeks to shoot, that's $1.875 million a week until the wrap party, minus the percentages taken by your team.

2. Your manager: 15 percent. By law, your manager cannot make deals on your behalf. But the manager is the only person on your team concentrating on your long-term career goals and earning potential. Your manager also retains responsibility for your "triple threat" cred, ensuring that, if you do not technically fit the definition of a "triple threat," you soon will. A good manager can also help pinpoint your requisite silly, semidisgusting ability, such as folding your tongue to look like an origami mantis. Do not underestimate the value or necessity of the silly, semidisgusting ability. You can't get a *Vanity Fair* writer to write about how authentic and down-to-Earth you are for a Hollywood powerhouse if you can't at least fart "The Star-Spangled Banner" over burgers at the Four Seasons.[55]

3. Your business manager: 5 percent. This person pays all major bills on your behalf, handles your accounting and taxes, and sometimes even recommends and monitors investments and, if necessary, puts you on a monthly allowance. Good business managers will also help create "personal services" or "loan out" companies in your name to save you 15 to 50 percent on your tax bills.

4. Tax collectors: Not technically members of your support staff, but no doubt fans of your work. Unfortunately for them, most will never meet you, but they will process the estimated **50 to 60 percent** of your paycheck that goes to state, local, and federal taxes, plus social security. Yes, you are allowed to deduct business expenses, so you may end up paying less than 50 percent, but according to tax experts to the stars, 50 percent is the ceiling. We're being conservative, here.

5. Your people: Attorneys, house managers, assistants, publicists, chefs, nannies, nutritionists, and trainers all fall under this category, as does the occasional stylist or makeup artist—if the studio is being mean and refusing to pay for such necessities. Your people cost an estimated **10 percent** of your paycheck and charge weekly salaries, monthly stipends, or hourly rates.

---

[55] **Forget burping.** It's already taken by Cameron Diaz, who can pretty much burp on demand. Look it up on YouTube.

The Bigger Your Name, the Less You Should Pay

According to some Hollywood money experts, true A-list stars often pay less for their agents, publicists, and other members of their crack support team. In fact, rumor has it that some triple-A-list names don't pay anything. At all. If the worldwide recognizability of your name falls somewhere between McDonald's and Super Mario, try this for fun: March into your agent's office, seek him out among his forest of mini-bamboo waterfalls, and inform him that his new take from your projects is 0 percent. In exchange, you will stay on at his very lucky agency, which can drop your platinum-coated name in any conversation or sales pitch it wants. Your agent will cry. With joy, of course.

Emergency scenario:

You need a new $5,000 watch

Suppose the battery on your $5,000 watch dies and you need a new watch. Simply head to the nearest awards show gifting suite. There likely will be a new watch already preselected for you. Swag suites are also fine places to restock on clean underwear and bottles of champagne. Other necessaries gifted at awards show swag suites in recent years include diamond earrings, vacuum cleaners,[56] leather jackets, designer sunglasses, airline tickets, video game consoles, full-body laser-resurfacing treatments, cell phones packaged with a year's worth of free calls, Botox and other wrinkle-banishing treatments, weekend stays at the Ritz-Carlton, one-year gym memberships, pearl necklaces, and French lingerie.

A Word of Encouragement

After paying off your taxes and your percentages to all of your team members, you may find yourself taking home only 10 or 15 percent of your original paycheck. Fight the urge to wallow in resentment or anger. That's still about $1.5 million—probably more than Justin Timberlake gets, that koala-faced punk.

Justin Timberlake, punk-ass.

[56] **Vacuum cleaner:** A device that sweeps particulate matter, such as wayward Swarovski crystals and unruly Vicodins, off the floor.

Receiving Your Due:
All about Swag

Publicists estimate that A-listers can easily receive at least $25,000 worth of tribute per awards show, between the gifts presented at swag suites and the thank-you packages offered to show presenters. Publicists also admit this is a conservative figure. Between the Oscars, the Emmys, the Grammys, and various MTV and Nickelodeon jammity-jam awards, you should command a yearly tribute of at least the low to mid six figures. If you fear image dilution by showing up at the swag suites yourself, go ahead and send your stylist or assistant. She will haul everything back to your compound atop her wiry, size-two frame, with a smile on her face and a song on her lips. Reward her with whatever free lip gloss you find in the goodie bags. She's so worth it.

If you decide to go yourself, make sure that the suite people have customized the space to your needs before you arrive. Before Prince steps into a backstage lounge—gifting or otherwise—he requires the lights to be dimmed, all music to be silenced, and the room to be completely cleared. Even other celebrities must go. He also allows no one to speak to him unless spoken to. Consider establishing a list of similarly reasonable requests. It will greatly reduce the stress that comes with all that free pampering.

★★★★A-List Tip

What Your Stack of Freebies Says about You

Top gifting gurus say true A-listers receive at least $20,000 a month in free, unsolicited gifts. The gifts usually come in the form of designer clothes, shoes, handbags, and cosmetics from media-savvy publicists. They can also include cars or car leases, offers for hotel stays, and vouchers for cosmetic surgery. A sudden drop below $15,000 in monthly gifts could indicate a serious loss of stardom. Consult your publicist immediately.

Emergency scenario:

Some clown thinks he can take your photo just because you're at a celebrity gifting suite being covered by the press

Beware the stealth sniper attacks that often await A-listers at swag suites. The most dangerous trap comes from gifters asking your permission for a photo, usually posing with the product they are giving away. A soap or reality star may not see this as a very large price to pay in exchange for a $30,000 necklace of pearls from the South Seas, but they are wrong. Seeing your carefully crafted image trapped in a room devoid of soft-fill lighting and other basic human rights is a very, very high price to pay, and you simply will not pay it. Then turn on your heel and leave. The gifters will still give you the item, and they'll apologize, to boot.

A Warning about Taxes

Recently the brownshirted people of the United States Internal Revenue Service have begun to cast their covetous nearsighted eyes upon the gifts you receive yearly. Unlike in years past, when expensive gifts could be written off by the corporate givers as "promotional expenses," the taxpaying onus has, increasingly, shifted to you and your fellow Olympians in the creative community. If you receive thousands and thousands of dollars' worth of swag yearly—and as an A-lister, you surely do—you are probably going to have to pay taxes on them.

Bruce Willis

Unless you invest in a restaurant.

In general, top celebrity finance guys deal in two kinds of investments—tax-free bonds, which are boring, and restaurants, which are fun and exciting. In opening a restaurant, you will grace an elite club already populated by many other, lesser celebrities, such as Bruce Willis, Robert De Niro, Ashton Kutcher, Justin Timberlake, and Jennifer Lopez. All of those good people have invested in eateries at one time or another.

If your restaurant is profitable, hey, terrific. If it isn't, your financial advisor may be able to, theoretically, count those losses against the gains you made in swag, essentially zeroing out that income. Make your accountant's day: Call him an hour or so before his son's championship soccer match and tell him

he's taking you to Nobu right now for some sushi. Then, after he's bought you and your entourage a few rounds of sake, slip in the restaurant suggestion. He'll love it so much he'll cry. And not, as he might insist between blubbers, because his son is growing up without a daddy.

Cashing in on Your Fame: Making a Living without Shooting That Crap Michael Bay Blockbuster

Naturally, many people also wish to pay you to add class to their event. Say an entertainment marketer wants you to attend a swag suite and take the gifts while a preapproved photographer takes some staged publicity photos. Perhaps a club impresario or art dealer or boutique owner has begged you to "host" a grand opening gala.

Whatever the event is, you shouldn't even leave your gated compound unless pay is involved. A typical A-list "hosting" fee starts at about $50,000 and requires a signed contract from both parties. In exchange for the money, you typically are required to show up—not necessarily on time—and work the carpet and VIP room for about two hours. You may have to pose with the real hosts and perhaps one or two reps from the party's liquor sponsor, but additional hours are extra. Under no circumstances should you have to mingle with—or even party in sight of—the rest of the riffraff at the event. There is nothing in the dictionary that says hosts have to be visible to guests.

If the event does not involve charity, you may also require the event planners to accommodate your entourage. Most planners earmark a cost of about $10,000 to go toward making you and your entourage happy for the evening.

But for the sake of professionalism, keep your clique small. Event planners start to get tetchy if you bring more than six friends.

If you crave still more cash, no problem. Since the first edition of this book went to press, a booming industry has emerged that requires little more than you walking up and down a red carpet and reciting designer names. Alls you have to do is wear a necklace, earrings, bracelet or gown from a certain designer, and that designer will pay you six to seven figures for your graciousness. The practice has been going on since at least the early 2000s, when Halle Berry, according to an insider, got paid $50,000 to wear a Bulgari necklace during the Oscars. On the afternoon of the Oscars, go-betweens stood out on a Los Angeles street corner with a paper bag containing the necklace and the $50,000. Berry's limousine arrived. The car window opened. The go-betweens stuck the bag through the limo window, Berry snatched up the goods, and the driver took off.

Since then, actresses have upped their asking price and, presumably, ditched the paper sacks. Based on his experiences competing for

Halle Berry

neckline space, famed jeweler Martin Katz told me that current jewelry-placement payouts range from $100,000 to $750,000—the reported amount that Anne Hathaway earned for wearing Tiffany to the 2011 Oscars. Your BFF Gwyneth Paltrow allegedly got $500,000 from Louis Vuitton to wear that house's jewelry on the same night. The following year, Paltrow's fee apparently doubled; Vanity Fair reports that Chinese jewelry designer Anna Hu paid the actress $1 million to wear a single diamond cuff to the 2012 Oscars. (Representatives for both actresses have denied the reports about the 2011 show.)

Emergency Scenario:
You Must Pay for Something

Everyone in this business, including publicists for Badgley Mischka and other celebrity-friendly fashion houses, is a human being. At one point someone is bound to forget your basic right to receive most items for free or at a deep discount. Someone may even accidentally send you some sort of bill and ask you to pay it. You will know the bill by its thin, paperlike texture, and a column of numbers indicating "costs" of an item and what you "owe." [60]

A call to your own publicist should clear this silliness up in no time. In some extreme circumstances you may be forced to actually pay for an item—a meal, for example, or a car. No one, not even incredible Hollywood legend Morgan Freeman (SUCH an honor to work with) can predict when or where these crises may emerge. Nonetheless, there is no excuse for being unprepared. At the very least, have a plan ready for any stealth restaurant check that may worm itself into your trembling hands.

The most common A-list method for combating a sudden "bill" involves your credit card. The hardy, hobbitlike peoples in other parts of the coun-

---

[60] **For a quaint** slice of Americana, consult the glossary for definition of "cost."

try also use credit cards. Their plastic versions usually come in childlike palettes of blue, green, or gold. Your own elite card mostly likely comes in black and has a small picture of a fancifully helmeted Roman warrior. American Express calls it a "Centurion." To find it, open your wallet and seek out a small, dark square with the telltale Roman mummer in the center and your name on the bottom.[61] You will

Did we mention what an honor it is to work with Morgan Freeman?

know your AmEx black card by the delightful tinny sound it makes when thrown against a makeup artist's head; AmEx Black Cards are made of titanium.

There is no need to handle this odd device any longer than a few seconds. Hand the card to your assistant—or throw it at her head for repeat confirmation that you indeed have an AmEx Black Card. The assistant will then hand the card to a waitperson or clerk. Field reports indicate that A-listers like you rarely hand off the card themselves and instead use go-betweens when dealing with outsiders, even outsiders standing only a few feet from them.

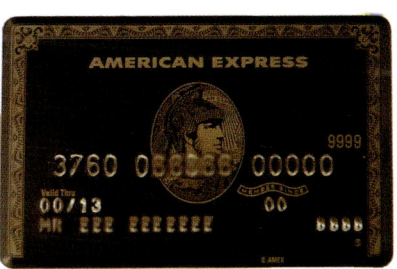

---

[61] This is not a "credit," even though the item in question is a "credit card."

Profiting From Pain

What to Charge for a Charity Event

Don't ever stop to wonder whether the universe has stacked itself against you. If you've ever been forced by a crowd of reverential fans to stop and sign autographs on the way into Mr. Chows, you already know the answer is yes. There are all those press people profiting from your private pain, all the time! Even when you didn't leak the existence of that pain to the press yourself!

There are ways to even out the odds that the stars have aligned against you. You can profit from someone else's pain.

Charge for charity appearances. All of them. Unless the gig is affiliated with your own self-named fundraising foundation or pet pity cause, charge your full appearance fee. Don't for a minute feel guilty. Famous people do the same thing about 99 percent of the time. So have Paris Hilton and Snoop Dogg.

Roughly 99 percent of the time, your fellow stars are doing the exact same thing. And they're pocketing the cash.

The logic they often offer, according to talent bookers, is that they get so many requests from charities—more than one hundred a year—that the stars can't possibly accommodate them all. So they pick the most worthy and organized—charities serious enough to have an event budget.

And don't stop there. A-listers routinely require charities to pay for travel, food, and any other expenses associated with their fund-raiser appearance. How are you supposed to muster the energy to raise thousands of dollars for starving Ugandan refugees if you didn't get decent room service the night before?

Navigating Your Simpering "Partners" in Fashion and Whatnot

At no point is life crueler than when you begin to attract multimillion-dollar endorsement contracts: A department store

cosmetics line is begging to throw you a few million for the right to name a lipstick after you. Maybe a French luggage company insists on making you their "face." As an A-list celebrity, you are expected to juggle at least three or four of these contracts. Typically, an A-lister has, as a foundation, a standing deal with one luxury fashion house (such as Jennifer Lawrence's recent tryst with Dior) and one beauty brand (like Halle Berry modeling for Revlon). On top of that, you can also juggle a jewelry gig, like Charlize did for Raymond Weil.

No one warned you about the downsides. Back when you were just another autistic gay evil-twin teenage character on *One Life to Live*, no one

To our knowledge, Charlize did not charge the designer before she donned this dress. I have no idea what she was thinking.

told you just how hard it can be to remember every single pan-European conglomerate that has you on its payroll.

You must find a way to keep track of each of your "partners." You must. Especially when you visit gifting suites during awards season. Getting your picture taken at a Revlon booth while under contract with L'Oréal may be a fundamental freedom, available to every man, woman, and child in the greater United States, but you signed away that right when you first agreed to utter "I'm worth it" for a paltry $5 million or so.[57] Now, if you get caught at the wrong place at the wrong time—say, at a Revlon party—your seemingly benevolent "partners" can sue you, for millions.

It gets worse. Once those fey luxury company CEOs have you on their payroll, they think they own you. Those French

---

[57] **The abuses don't end there.** According to the contract Beyoncé signed with L'Oréal, she had to work for ten whole days a year. If the company wanted her to work any extra days, she could only charge a paltry $25,000 per. Also stipulated in the contract, which was later obtained by The Smoking Gun, L'Oréal got to inspect Beyoncé's hair—whenever it wanted—with only two weeks' notice! Classy like she is, Beyoncé never complained.

Gwyneth Paltrow at the 83rd Academy Awards, wearing Louis Vuitton jewelry.

Anne Hathaway wearing a Tiffany necklace at the 83rd Academy Awards.

luggage people will not stop caravaning up to your home, laden with bottomless piles of free duffel bags handcrafted in the mountains of Italy, never once stopping to consider that you might be a vegan, or that you be suffering the early symptoms of gratitude fatigue.[58]

Soon you find yourself fleeing from the crushing adoration of it all, cowering in your bathtub while your assistant lights candles and cradles your head. Now you know why Charlize Theron[59] always seems to have a slightly hollow look behind those veldt-toughened blue eyes. It's the endorsements. They totally, totally break you.

Jennifer Lawrence in Dior at the 85th Academy Awards.

[58] **When Jennifer Lopez worked** as a spokesmodel for Louis Vuitton, she reportedly helped herself to thousands of dollars' worth of the merchandise. She could have thrown her back out carrying it all, but did anyone think of that? No. No they did not.

[59] Theron's endorsement deal with Swiss watchmaker Raymond Weil soured after she sported a Dior watch in a separate ad for Dior perfume. Weil sued Theron for unspecified damages. The suit was later settled.

Combating a "Bill" via Remote

At one point you are bound to be billed in absentia. Seamier entrepreneurs delight in siccing an outstanding balance on you when you are far away and unable to defend yourself. Most often these predators will attempt to bill you through your assistant, most often when she has embarked on errands alone, a child in the jungle with no megastar to help her defend against unwarranted charges to your person.

Under no circumstances should your assistant leave your compound without specific training to combat this very emergency. With practice, your assistant should easily tackle any expense, in your name, in a matter of seconds—and do it the A-list way.

True stars train their assistants to precisely mimic their signatures. This is the norm among the fabulous. In other words, your assistant should visit stores or other vendors on your behalf, whip out your credit card, and sign your name in your stead. Any boutique clerk worth his sea

★★★★A-List Tip

What You Have in Common with That Little Man Who Drives You to the Set

Like your driver, you also can get paid just to zip around in a car all day. Whenever you land a celebrity endorsement deal with a major carmaker, the client will usually throw in a free auto or at least a complimentary lease. If the client forgets to do that and instead tries to sneak off after merely handing you a $25 million check, please remember to maintain your aura of enlightened professionalism. Maybe these folks are from out of town or something. Simply remind your manager to remind the carmaker that a talent of your caliber really comes along but once in a lifetime, and that kind of talent is best reflected in a brand-new Mercedes Two-door SL convertible.

salt facial masks will recognize the assistant as your distinguished emissary and accept the signature as yours without question or hassle.[62]

As for what stars actually buy with their credit cards, and for how much, the general rule is that anything under $1,000 usually calls for cash, while larger payments require a credit card.

Make certain that your assistant has mastered your signature to your satisfaction. Matching the weight and angle of each stroke is not enough. Do not let her leave for the day until she has captured all the spirit and ethereal vitality that critics have hailed, in your work, time and again, as a winning combination unique to modern filmmaking.

[62] **Having a signature** doppelgänger also works well when you need to sign a bunch of photos or memorabilia. As your fellow A-listers know, an assistant's signature works just as well as the celebrity's when providing autographs through the mail. The can also prevents perilous cases of hand cramp. To date, no star has ever died of hand cramp, but then again, before St. Laurent, no one had ever died of fabulousness.

Purchasing a New Home

A-list status entitles you to receiving most necessities for free or at a noteworthy discount. For example, fashion publicists can supply every element of your wardrobe—including underwear—for free, along with makeup, personal care products, pet supplies, home decor, and household appliances. On-set doctors provide most basic medical care for free, and your Screen Actors Guild insurance can handle the rest. However, one element remains stubbornly out of reach for even the most resplendent of men and women in your class: homes. Insiders say that famous people often purchase permanent dwellings in the same manner as everyday groundlings—with a mortgage or, if possible and desirable, with cash. A good financial advisor will instruct you to buy under a business name or corporation, to protect you from prying paparazzi or home-related lawsuits.

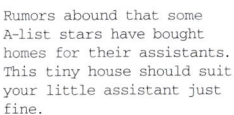
Rumors abound that some A-list stars have bought homes for their assistants. This tiny house should suit your little assistant just fine.

Life-Threatening Disasters

Murder Trials, Jail Stints, Emergency Evacuations, and the Enemies within Your Own Head

As isolated and well-patrolled as your new home may be, it is never safe enough. From anything. Of course, Hollywood is rife with stories of obsessive fans who go too far. Most fall under the "harmless" category—benighted child-men eager only to smell your wardrobe or cradle a few stray hairs from your favorite weave—but still others pose undeniable danger. Some may wish to maim you, kill you, or even through your high school yearbook to see what your first nose looked like.

Don't forget to buy some space for your staffers. Before their announced divorce, Madonna and Guy Richie owned a reported six homes in London, including two just for employees.

You may think yourself safe after building fresh barricades. After all, your ten-foot-high reclaimed slate water wall fountain—impeccably designed by your good friend and architecture fancier Brad Pitt—seems too high and too slippery to scale. That's exactly the kind of complacency that can catapult your compound from a happy home into a seething standoff in a matter of minutes.

Besides, even if your high walls, security cameras, disorienting infinity pools, and ex-Mossad security goons do manage to protect you from outsiders, those outsiders are still … outside. As soon as you emerge in your tinted SUV, or tinted enviro-car, or tinted Maybach, the photographers will be there, waiting to follow you to your favorite Starbucks.

The point: If your security team isn't trained to ponder every invasion scenario, no matter how small or ridiculous, fire them at once.[63]

---

[63] **And, again,** fire your publicist.

When You Must Flee the Compound

If Charlie Sheen has booked all of the qualified security personnel in your area, and you have no gun with which to shoot an intruder[64], you have one more option at your disposal: Flight. Find the nearest Maybach or Ferrari, hop in, and leave, bivouacking at the Raffles L'Ermitage hotel until you have regained your nerves and can begin to plan your move to a new permanent home.

If you have to leave your home, you have to do it right. Many of your less fortunate colleagues—such as those trapped in the daytime drama demimonde—would simply run from the area and never return, leaving behind their most precious possessions. But you have no way of sustaining yourself without your two Pilates reformer machines. Science also has yet to weigh in on whether children of famous parents can survive for more than a few hours outside a custom nursery equipped with $8,300 Versailles-style cribs. Don't be a hero. Have your assistant book a moving company, one with experience in evacuating A-listers like you.

Companies such as NorthStar, which counts Angelina Jolie as a client, pride themselves on accommodating famous people at very short notice. They also will not make eye contact with you

Sure, Charlie Sheen needs security people, but you need them more. Never forget that.

or your children without your prior permission and can arrive at any time, day or night, to pack and move your

---

[64] See page 152 for instructions on shooting a paparazzo without suffering arrest or punishment.

things.[65]

Proper A-list moving companies also have trained their workers in deflecting paparazzi bribes and deploying multiple decoy trucks to thwart tabloid recon missions. Also do not hire a moving company unless they retain their own squadrons of nannies, pet sitters, and organizers to meet any unlikely factors you may have forgotten, such as your children. Movers-to-the-stars offer these upgraded services to A-listers like you as a matter of course.

Once the workers have packed up the compound and have touched down at the new location, your celebrity moving company will unpack and arrange every single thing you own in an exact reproduction of your old home. Movers often take preauthorized photos of your home—every closet, every mirror—for reference during the unpacking process. Inspect your new bunker carefully for mistakes. Once satisfied, make sure the movers return not only the prints of the photos but also any negatives or disk drives containing the images. Magazines will pay thousands for a similar peek into your fantasy walk-in closets—but only if they're exclusive and properly lit.

---

[65] **According to NorthStar,** one of its celebrity clients wanted no reminder that his ex was moving out of his home. But he wasn't willing to leave his home during the moveout either. So whenever the celebrity wanted to enter a room occupied by the movers, the NorthStar crew had to remove all evidence of their existence—including themselves—and then resume their work once the celebrity had passed through.

Emergency Scenario:

A Chair Is Bothering You

According to NorthStar, the celebrity moving company, you are not the first star to face down this problem. Assuming you are in your home when this happens, your first priority should be to regain calm. Close your eyes and imagine yourself a few miles away, in your backyard, surrounded by whispering palms and your squadron of adoring pugs. Only after your heartbeat has returned to normal should you even consider squaring off against the offending chair. Facing the chair at all times, reach for the telephone, call your mover, and demand that someone come to your home and move the piece of furniture to another room at once. The mover will gladly deploy a rep immediately, day or night, to move the chair into the other room. NorthStar wouldn't say which celebrity once called them to move a single chair like this, but that's not important. The key thing here is that the celebrity was A-OK.

Getting Away with Murder

A Guide to Knowing When to Fire

At one point or another you may just have to shoot someone. Perhaps the paparazzi have violated your right to control your image one too many times, or your publicist failed to properly insulate you from a bad day. Time to shoot, and not with your phone, either. Do not even hesitate for a single second. According to several studies conducted for this purpose of this reference guide, no A-list celebrity has ever suffered a conviction for murder.

The same cannot be said for other breeds of celebrity, however. Not sons of celebrities. Not parents, not ladies' maids who think they're famous, not spouses, siblings, coaches, handmaidens, coke dealers, or the Dude Who Watches the Car While We Up in the Club. Unlike you, those folk all carry serious risk of jail time if convicted of killing someone.[66]

According to attorneys and other court types, two major factors stand between you and a guilty verdict for murder: universal, unconditional love from millions of people, and money.

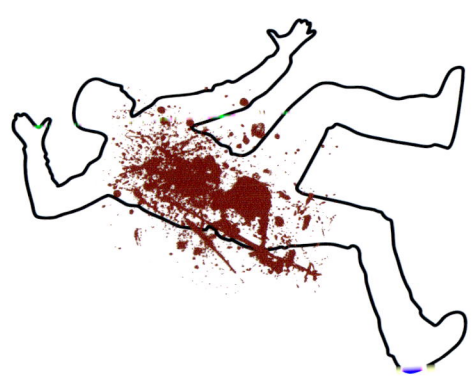

[66] **See more** on the guy who watches the car while we up in the club on page 29.

You can make $200,000 in a single day if you needed to. Paris Hilton reportedly charged $200,000 to celebrate her twenty-fourth birthday at a Las Vegas nightclub. Your good pal Owen Wilson was charging $100,000 about 10 years ago; now, if your business manager accounts for inflation and the fact that of course you certainly are no Owen Wilson, you easily could charge double that. In fact, consider charging closer to a half-million dollars—Halle Berry's appearance fee just a few short years ago, if you believe the media. If you feel a sudden pang of remorse at asking so much, then here: Usher has charged a reported $150,000.[67]

Even without the massive cash wad you'll pay for experts, you'll need even more for attorneys. If you have not paid for a single pair of shoes in the past six years,[68] you probably have more than enough for the legal team.

Now, for your second big advantage: you. Most Americans live under the delusion that they somehow know you, having seen you on TV or in films for years and years. They see you as a kind of friend, making it much more difficult to jail you. As Cristina Pérez, judge and host of the TV show *Cristina's Court*, once told me, "The benefit of being a celebrity in these cases is that we grew up with them. Robert Blake was Baretta, someone people grew up with. It's hard for a jury to convict someone they have known all their lives."

So, fuck it. Pull the trigger. Just don't forget to charge top dollar for the tell-all book.

Fact: A poor person who is assigned a public defender might get $250 to $500 from the state to spend money on expert witnesses, but Phil Spector allegedly spent $200,000 just on witnesses who testified in court. Don't even try to calculate that gap. Let me do that for you. It's a difference of $199,750.

---

[67] **For more on earning** without ever having to report for a 6 AM makeup call again, see 125.

[68] Trick question. Of course you haven't paid for any shoes in the past six years.

Shooting a Paparazzo

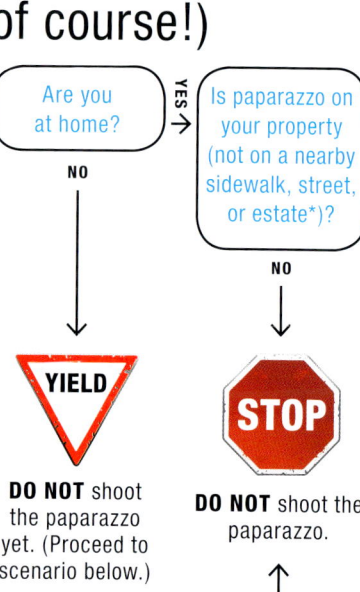

(in self-defense, of course!)

Are you at home? — YES → **Is paparazzo on your property (not on a nearby sidewalk, street, or estate*)?** — YES → **Has paparazzo expressly refused to vacate your property?** — YES → According to California jury instructions, you may now use "reasonable force" to eject the paparazzo. If your ex-Mossad bodyguard** is off celebrating Hanukkah or Yom Kippur, call the police or brandish a hose or air gun, which will likely merit an all-clear from Johnny Law. Or, if you still prefer to use lethal force, continue....

NO ↓

YIELD

DO NOT shoot the paparazzo yet. (Proceed to scenario below.)

↓

Are you in a public place? — YES → **Do you have a specific location you are trying to reach?** — YES → **Has the paparazzo blocked access to your desired location?**

NO ↓ (under "Is paparazzo on your property")

STOP

DO NOT shoot the paparazzo.

↑ NO

NO ↓ (under "Has paparazzo expressly refused")

STOP

DO NOT shoot the paparazzo.

↑ NO

If your paparazzo is British

England is a relatively gun-free country, with only 5.6 guns per 100 people. (The United States has 90 guns per 100 people.) If your paparazzo is British, he may not

recognize your gun as a weapon. In a loud, clear voice, say, "Oi, wanker, I'm tooled up enough to slot you, innit?" This should serve as sufficient warning to a British paparazzo in his native tongue.

If you must hit the paparazzo with your car

If your escape requires hitting the paparazzo with your car, try to run over only the feet. Britney Spears has reportedly run over three pairs of feet—two pairs belonging to paparazzi, and one to a sheriff's deputy. No charges have ever been filed.

Did you know?

At one point during a Malibu baby shower for Britney Spears in 2005, a paparazzo stationed on a nearby property looked down and discovered the following facts: (a) there was some sort of pellet lodged in his leg (b) the pellet had come from a BB gun, and (c) the shooter seemed to have been stationed somewhere very near where Spears was getting festooned with $80 baby blankets. No charges were filed in the incident.

Has paparazo made physical threats and/or brandished a weapon?*** → **YES** → Has paparazzo indicated he is a soldier of fortune, ninjas or paid assasin intent on doing you bodily harm? → **YES** → **SHOOT THE PAPARAZZO.** *BANG!*

NO ↓

STOP

DO NOT shoot the paparazzo.

↑ **NO**

Are you unable to avoid paparazzo, because he is agile or fat? → **YES** →

NO ↓

STOP

DO NOT shoot the paparazzo.

↑ **NO**

Have you asked the fat and/or agile paparazzo to move out of your way? → **YES** →

NO ↓

STOP

DO NOT shoot the paparazzo.

↑ **NO**

Has the fat and/or agile paparazzo refused to move? → **YES** →

USE A NOXIOUS SPRAY such as vinegar on paparazzo. Pepper spray may result in an assult charge and is not recommended.

---

* **Legal Fact:** Having your ex-Mossad bodyguard assert that a land parcel is your property when it actually is not your property does not constitute legal owerniship.

** For fun, you may send your ex-Mossad bodyguard out onto the lawn to threaten the paparazzo as he flees.

***Unless the paparazzo has a bayonet, Taser, or other harmful mechanism attached to his lens or focus ring, cameras do not count as weapons.

It's Not Like I Killed Someone:
Shoplifting, DUIs, and Other Misunderstandings

As often as you tend to forget this, let me remind you: You are a human being. You make mistakes. Just as a humble clerk at the Gramercy Park Hotel may accidentally put on the wrong Narciso Rodriguez uniform one morning, you might unwittingly walk out of a Saks store with $5,000 in designer clothes that don't belong to you. Or maybe you forget to not do cocaine one day, and instead make the very understandable mistake of *doing* cocaine. Or you just have the misfortune of having another car sitting in front of you while you are driving very fast.

Never fear. If you're a true movie star, then go ahead. Snort the coke. Hit the car. The courts understand completely that your brain works on a highly creative level and can't always discern minutiae like criminal statutes. Winona Ryder served not one day in prison stemming from her 2001 shoplifting arrest. Instead she was sentenced to three years' probation and 480 hours of community service. In 2001, Halle Berry fled the

Community service beats jail. After all, you get fresh air and meet "regular" people.

scene of a car accident before police arrived, spurring a misdemeanor charge. She also got probation.

Yes, Kiefer Sutherland did forty-eight days in the hoosegaw stemming from a DUI (see more in the next section), and Robert Downey Jr. did a year after he failed to report for a court-ordered drug test. But their most important asset—their fame—has not diminished in the least. And the jail that Sutherland stayed in was actually a pretty cool jail.

Robert Downey Jr, reformed bad boy and wearer of fabulous glassses.

You also have no reason to worry about your bank account. Lawyer fees for minor brushes with the law—even for a leading figure such as you—are pretty low. At the least, you'll pay perhaps $5,000, at the most an estimated $50,000, according to top celebrity lawyer Larry Stein. "Not big, big dollars," he assures. And that's true. For you, those are *microscopic* dollars.

Choosing a Jail

You probably cannot imagine yourself spending even one night in jail. Neither can anybody else. A-list stars rarely, if ever, enter a jail unless the jail is on a soundstage. If you ever find yourself sentenced to a jail term, even for a misdemeanor or very minor conviction, check with your agent to confirm your per-film fee; you may, unbeknownst to you, actually be a B-lister.[69]

Most of the celebrities who have served time in jail fall considerably below your caliber in the Hollywood hierarchy. In social terms, they probably wouldn't make it as far as your stylists' front door. However, for your amusement, a list of jailed so-not A-listers follows:

[69] **Sorry to be** the one to break it to you, Mr. Snipes. No use glaring at me like that. I know you're not a real vampire.

Jailed so-not A-listers

- Lil' Kim, who served about ten months in a Philadelphia prison for conspiracy and perjury and a wardrobe disturbing to the peace.

- Paris Hilton, who did twenty-three days after a violating a parole order.

- Robert Downey Jr., jailed for a year in state prison for missing a court-ordered drug test. Downey may be the most successful actor ever to serve that much time in jail, but it should be noted that the year was 1999, even before he was cast in *Ally McBeal.*

- Michelle Rodriguez, who died in a zombie movie, and had a part in that show about that thing before getting busted on a probation something or other.

- Nicole Richie, convicted on a DUI and sent to a prison in a Los Angeles suburb while four months pregnant. Though she sported brunette hair for her mug shot and switched to blonde for her jail booking photo, relentless reporters somehow saw through the ruse and blew the whole event wide open.

- Lindsay Lohan, who attended the same jail as Richie but may or may not have pledged the same branch of the Latin Queens

- Mike Tyson, for driving without a neck[70].

- **Martha Stewart, who got five months** in a Virginia prison for lying to federal investigators, but really. She should go right back in there if she doesn't stop nagging your publicist about you guesting on her show.

Martha Stewart

The only recent jail alumnus who even comes close to your level is Kiefer Sutherland. Sutherland used to date your colleague Julia Roberts, and he has made a few films, and you hear through your manager that his TV show does quite well, which makes you happy because Donald Sutherland was one of your mentors, and you wish his whole family nothing but the best, and you know that because your assistant says that on every card he sends to Donald on your behalf.

Kiefer really has nothing to offer you in terms of movie packaging, but his jail experience can teach you much should the justice system ever resolutely fail and consign you to the big house.[71] Sutherland did not attend a county prison, but, rather, then-$85-per-day "pay-to-stay" facility in Glendale, California. If your conviction is not for a violent crime, and if the judge

Kiefer Sutherland

allows it, you, too, may make a bid to stay in such a facility. The downside: no early releases for overcrowding or high charisma. Sutherland had to serve every minute of his forty-eight-day term, often held at the mercy of security guards who could speak to him whenever they wished. The facility also imposed a punitive rite known as "laundry"—heretofore reserved only for members of your household staff—and limited his phone calls to a ridiculously short fourteen minutes at a time.

Such government-operated facilities do have advantages; should you choose to stay in one, you will avoid unclean or overcrowded surroundings; you will likely have your own cell; and, if you serve in a town like Pasadena or Fullerton, you may leave for work during the day and return at night.

However, do not underestimate the advantages of county jails. You stand a much higher chance of early release at an overcrowded county facility.

---

[70] Technically not accurate, but very well could be by press time.

[71] *Big house*: Colorful jailbird slang for "prison." Although the typical modern penal facility is nowhere near as "big" a "house" as your sprawling Hollywood Hills summer estate. Criminals are known exaggerators and prevaricators. That's why they are in prison.

Donatella Versace

Non-famous convicts sent to Los Angeles county jails generally serve only 10 percent of their sentences because of overcrowding. However, recent field studies indicate that celebrities who check into the same county facilities spend even less time than that. After all, such jails have relatively little experience with the steady media siege you bear every waking minute of your incredible life, and you cannot blame them if they choose to jettison you at the earliest possible moment.

Some math: In 2007, Nicole Richie was sentenced to four days for a DUI. That's ninety-six hours. Ten percent of that is 9.6 hours. Richie ended up serving eighty-two minutes. Lohan checked into jail for a twenty-four-hour sentence in 2007. Ten percent of that would be 2.4 hours. She served eighty-four minutes. Rodriguez, however, served about eighteen days of a 180-day sentence due to overcrowding—exactly 10 percent.

Another possible benefit to entering a jail for the masses: Unlike pay-to-stay hoosegows, county facilities may end up squirreling you away into a "special needs unit" for celebrities or the like, where you will get a cell all to yourself—without having to pay an outrageous, $85-per-day fee. Party giraffe Paris Hilton scored herself a special-needs-unit cell during her three-week stay at the Century Regional Detention Facility, near Los Angeles, in 2007. And she isn't even particularly tight with Donatella Versace.

Besides, on the off chance that you contract a staph infection while in lockup, you can always leverage that into a magazine cover story as did your good friend Rosie O'Donnell, who isn't really your good friend, but it just isn't worth it to piss her off.

Jailhouse Math

- The accused: Nicole Richie
- The sentence: 4 days for DUI = 96 hours
- The math: 10% of 96 hours = 9.6 hours
- The reality: 82 minutes

- The accused: Lindsay Lohan
- The sentence: 24 hours for DUI and cocaine charges
- The math: 10% of 24 hours = 2.4 hours
- The reality: 84 minutes

Emergency Scenario:

Your Inner Voice Is Frightening You

Along with ever-present threats from overeager justicemongers, still more perils hang over every A-lister. One of the deadliest foes you face lurks deep within, and not within your production office, though there's no telling what kind of nonorganic garbage the maintenance people keep spraying on your peace lilies.

No, your biggest enemy often lies within you own luminous head. We speak, of course, of your *inner voice.*

Your colleagues love to talk about their "inner voice," also known as gut instinct. The "inner voice" is terrific for improving your acting, and it can, on occasion, help you cry on command. But in truth, the inner voice is just as often a hazard as it is a help and should be ignored in nearly all instances.

For example, suppose your agent doesn't call you back within his usual six-minute window. That is definitely, absolutely, *not* the time to be relying on the inner voice. (See Script, next.)

Remember the last time that happened?

Fade In:

YOU

Hmmm. I just called CAA, and my agent's second assistant said he was in a meeting. He *never* does that. He's usually so eager to take my call, and then we talk about my unique gift for at least *forty-five minutes*. You don't think he's dumping me, do you?

INNER VOICE

Let's be reasonable. How long ago did you call?

YOU

Ten minutes, I think?

INNER VOICE

Oh. Ouch. Forget I said anything.

YOU

I know, right? I said it was—wait, what?

INNER VOICE

Was it Sandy Bullock who once waited 10 minutes for her agent to call her back? Can't remember. But it may as well have been. Did you SEE *All About Steve?*

YOU

God no.

INNER VOICE

Be glad you didn't. I did and my eyes exploded.

YOU

You're not helping my anxiety disorder.

INNER VOICE

You have anxiety disorder? Oh, man. Agents hate
that. I wouldn't be surprised if what's-her-name
had an anxiety disorder, you know, the one that
CAA dumped last week?

YOU

Who?

INNER VOICE

Exactly.

YOU

I think my heart just started beating all kind of
fluttery. How do you know when you're having a
stroke?

INNER VOICE

Oh my God. DON'T have a stroke. Your face may get
lopsided. Audiences don't want to see gimps. Your
agent told me that yesterday.

                              YOU

Hold on a second. You talked to Seth? Did he say
anything about me?

                         INNER VOICE

Well, nothing per se. I mean unless you
count—never mind.

                              YOU

What? What did he say?

                         INNER VOICE

Wait. Are you or are you not having a stroke?

                              YOU

I don't know. Maybe? Yes?

                         INNER VOICE

Then nothing. Seth didn't say anything. At all.
About your crow's feet and falling Q rating with
the eighteen-through-twenty-four demographic.

Sound effect: THUNK.

                         INNER VOICE

Hello?

And... Scene. My point is this: When it comes to real life, do
yourself a solid: Track down your "inner voice," cut out its
imaginary tongue and let it gurgle to itself in an imaginary
corner.

A Cheat Sheet for Your Assistant to Read

1,200 (calories): The recommended intake allowance of food and drink for weight maintenance outside the A-list community.

A-lister: Any actor who can open a movie on name alone and who generally commands at least $10 million a picture. At least, that was the figure as of press time. You might want to check with your friend Will Smith.

Addorall: See "Addies."

Addies: Slang for Adderall, the go-to prescription upper of choice for Hollywood denizens looking to remain (a) awake, (b) slim, and (c) free of cocaine convictions. Technically formulated to treat attention deficit disorder, which you've never heard of, but which you totally have, in case your doctor decides to ask.

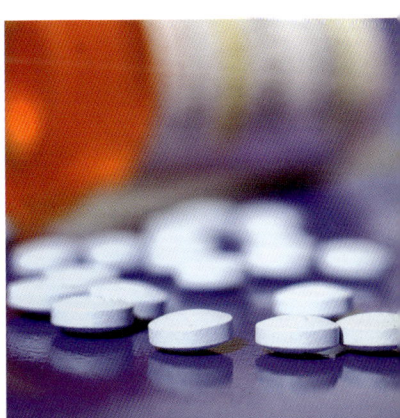

Agent: The person who secures work and negotiates contracts for a client performer, usually at a cost of 10 percent of a total paycheck.

Amazing: As an A-lister, the only adjective you really need to know, and one of the most popular descriptives in the business. Unlike wearing the same dress to an event, it's OK to use the "amazing" at the same time and place as a fellow A-lister; both Helen Mirren and Forest Whitaker were quoted as saying their Oscar runs were "amazing"—in the very same season—and no ill befell either of them.

Annie Leibovitz: Your good friend and family photographer. Has a day job shooting cute stuff for *Vanity Fair*.

Appearance fee/Hosting fee: What you charge to attend a party or event, such as a club opening or charity fund-raiser. A-lister appearance fees usually never fall under five figures.

Assistant: That person who keeps asking you how you want your soy latte. You pay her five figures for that, unless you've fired her by now. Also responsible for day-to-day tasks on your behalf, including autographs, signing your credit card slips, and interviewing potential nannies.

B-list: A catch-all term for less fortunate members of the acting community who command less than $10 million per film. Also refers to actors who have found themselves—either through cruel whim of fate or sad lack of inner brilliance—on a TV series.

Blackballing: A method by which a publicist kills a negative story by threatening to deny a reporter access to an entire roster of clients. Can go so far as banning news outlets from movie junkets, red-carpet premieres, and on-set visits.

Business manager: The little man who pays household expenses and vendor bills on your behalf, for a dizzying 5 percent of your pay.

C-list: Not really a list. But don't tell the *American Idol* contestant kids. They work hard and really ought to be on some sort of list.

Cost: The amount of money required for anyone outside the A-list community to obtain a good or service.

Exhaustion: According to doctors, not technically real. A symptom, not a sickness or disease, but nonetheless, your go-to excuse for checking into the hospital for illegal-drug overdose, prescription-drug overdose, or starvation.

Eye contact: An excellent bellwether for determining A-list status. If you can arrange, through your assistants, to ban all contact with your celebrated eyes while on the set, you are at least as famous as Jennifer Lopez, who has engaged in the same practice.

First Amendment: An insidious bit of wording allegedly found in the U.S. Constitution allowing anyone to say nearly anything about you at any time, without permission from you or your publicist. Easily quashed with blackballing. (See "Blackballing.")

First-dollar gross: Gross receipts from movie ticket sales from the first day on, before taxes and any other expenses. Pay based on first-dollar gross is the most desired type in the movie business—but for you, the A-lister, it's no problem.

Jury duty: A practice by which people outside the A-list community gather in temporary clans of twelve to determine the fate of someone on trial. Not a concern for people at your fame level.

Manager: The person responsible for building and sustaining your career over the long term. Coordinates appearances and projects and collaborates with your assistant to ensure your basic needs, such as all-white dressing rooms, are met. Usually takes 15 percent of your salary. Not to be confused with business manager.

Morgan Freeman: Amazing, just amazing. Such an honor to work with.

Opening a picture: Industryspeak for your rare ability to greenlight a film or sell movie tickets on your name alone.

Premiere: A private event disguised as a public gala by which your latest film debuts to press and select insiders. Attendance often falls under an actor's contractual duty to promote a film; you slog through them somehow.

Price tag: A small snippet of paper or adhesive indicating the "cost" of an item for people outside the A-list community. See "cost."

Production company or shingle: A small business, usually seeded by a large movie studio on your behalf, by which you screen potential scripts, option properties, and claim credit for all of it as a producer.

Publicist: The squat woman in the linen suit who engineers every key aspect of your public being; you pay with about $4,000 a month; she pays only with her soul. Responsible for booking and overseeing magazine cover shoots, press junkets, TV show visits, live appearances, red carpet looks, and for the planning and marketing of your weddings.

Stylist: The person hired to choose your wardrobe for all major public appearances, including awards shows, premieres, and movie junkets. Usually paid by a studio, or, if absolutely necessary, your own production company.

Jennifer Aniston's stylist is so good that his clients age backwards. If you have to ask how much, you cannot afford him.

Uni-naming: Taking elements of both names of a celebrity couple and forming a new term, such as "Brangelina."

Vagina: The chutelike delivery system by which most women outside the A-list community produce their children. Anatomical reference: Generally located in the same area that receives your twice-monthly bikini wax treatment at the Anastasia salon

With, And: Two particularly respectable flavors of film credit, as in "… and Judi Dench." Never, ever occurs by accident; always negotiated by your agent.

SOURCES

The author would like to thank the following friends and sources:

Rick Wellman, colorist extraordinaire
Pacific Pet Transport
Marc Malkin
Ted Casablanca
Brad Elterman, BuzzFoto.com
Helena Krodel, the Jewelry Information Center
Dr. Brent Moelleken
Luggage Free
Harmony Walton, The Bridal Bar
Suzanne Hansen, the Hollywood Nanny
NorthStar Moving Corp.
Jeff Wallner, Lighthouse Financial Group
Adriana Gallarzo
Association of Celebrity Personal Assistants
Gary Mansour, Avion
Pacific Pet Transport
Lash Fary, Distinctive Assets
Tina Dirmann
Howard Bragman, 15 Minutes PR
Sebastien Lagree, Pilates Plus
Gary Morgan, Splash News
Sherri Blum, CID, Jack and Jill Interiors
Macky Dancy, Dancy-Power Automotive Group
Michael Eisenberg, Eisenberg Financial Advisors
Antonio Almeida
Robert Tuchman, TSE Sports and Entertainment
Renee Young, Renee Young & Assoc.

ACKNOWLEDGMENTS

The author would like to thank the following people, without whom etc., etc.

1.. Designer LeAnna Weller Smith, for giving my book its irresistible, candy-like appeal.

2. Ann Treistman, my editor, who worked me and worked me until I was little more than a nub of carbon and black tar. But you asked to be in here, so wave at yourself!

3. My invisible assistant Clancy, with your implacable spirit and jaunty collection of plaid hats. One day, you will become a real boy. Mommy promises.

4. My agent. Oh, wait. I don't have one.

5. Whatever CAA agent signs me first after reading item No. 4

6. The "other folks" at Skyhorse Publishing, including Tony Lyons, Bill Wolfsthal, and Abigail Gehring. If Ann says you're real, then fine. I choose to believe.

7. And, of course, the entire E! building, for treating me like top-tier talent even though I look nothing like Seacrest.

PHOTO CREDITS

All Access Photo Agency: 27, 33, 40, 51 (top), 52 (bottom), 53, 62, 66, 70, 72, 87, 88, 112, 115, 116, 123, 133, 136 (bottom), 143, 143
Henry Flores/Buzz Foto: 15
iStockphoto: 16, 23, 25, 38, 56, 68, 82, 100, 113, 119, 139, 140, 144, 145, 160
Shutterstock Images: All remaining images.

NOTES